Praise for

PAYING IT FORWARD

'From the very first story about Peter, this book draws you into the extraordinary world of paying it forward. Josh makes the case – powerfully – that business and entrepreneurship must become systematic forces for good, tackling not just homelessness but the twin evils of environmental degradation and social inequality. It's a serious book – dealing with what Capitalism 2.0 might look like – but it is also deeply moving on a human level. I defy you to read the last chapter, "Sonny's Story", without a lump coming to your throat.'
Alan Jope, CEO of Unilever

'*Paying It Forward* wonderfully distils the passion and determination that it takes to be a social entrepreneur. Filled with remarkable people and illuminating stories, Josh "pays it forward" by revealing how we can all make a difference to our world and our fellow human beings.'
Dame Helen Mirren

'Josh Littlejohn is a remarkable man – who has achieved extraordinary things in a really short time. *Paying It Forward* is his inspirational manifesto for social change and an important practical manual for living a life filled with purpose. Josh reveals what it takes to be a social entrepreneur and how we can all use our skills and energy to change lives rather than just chase profits. Full of heart, honesty, humour, and genuinely helpful advice, *Paying It Forward* is an essential read for our times.'
Richard Curtis CBE

'Josh Littlejohn is a rockstar of social impact. From opening a local coffee shop in Edinburgh to staging The World's Big Sleep Out in New York, he has helped countless people. In an era where businesses put profit over people, and politicians offer platitudes but no real change to this system, *Paying It Forward* is a much-needed reminder about what is really important. Much more than an appeal to truly value each other – it's a manifesto for practical steps we need to take to enable this to happen.'
Irvine Welsh

'Josh Littlejohn is a brilliant entrepreneur who has poured his heart, soul and energy into helping others – with remarkable results. I have personally slept out for four years running as part of Josh's Big Sleep Out campaigns and, in doing so, got a tiny glimpse into the harsh realities of homelessness. *Paying It Forward* is a fantastic, must-read book for anyone who wants to learn how they can also channel their ambition into changing society for the better.'
Sir Chris Hoy

'Having been in Social Bite and witnessed, first-hand, the immeasurable difference that Josh has made to the lives of innumerable people, *Paying It Forward* is an urgent and unmissable call to action that shows how we can all "pay it forward" by dedicating a little more effort and energy into helping others. Read this brilliant book now and start making an impact in the world!'
Martin Compston

PAYING IT FORWARD

PAYING IT FORWARD

HOW TO BE A SOCIAL ENTREPRENEUR

Josh Littlejohn MBE

Heligo
Books

First published in the UK by Heligo Books
an imprint of Bonnier Books UK
4th Floor, Victoria House, Bloomsbury Square,
London, WC1B 4DA
England

Owned by Bonnier Books
Sveavägen 56, Stockholm, Sweden

Hardback – 978-1-78870-840-1
Trade paperback – 978-1-78870-888-3
Ebook – 978-1-78870-841-8
Audio – 978-1-78870-842-5

Cover designed by Nick Stearn
Typeset by IDSUK (DataConnection) Ltd,
Printed and bound by Clays Ltd, Elcograf, S.p.A.

1 3 5 7 9 10 8 6 4 2

Heligo Books is an imprint of Bonnier Books UK
www.bonnierbooks.co.uk

To my parents, for dealing me the best cards in life;
To Sukhi, my wife, best friend and greatest support;
To Jack, the best brother I could have ever asked for;
And to my son, Theodore, I hope you grow up to become yourself.

Foreword

Sometimes I wish I could be just like Josh Littlejohn. Then again more often I'm glad I'm not. I don't understand how you can live at such a pitch of engagement, be so effective, so collegiate in external manner and so very driven inside what must be a churning mind and a burning heart.

Anyway, he's brilliant. The stuff he does is mad. Stuff for other people. All the time. The stunts he has come up with are fantastic and always (here's the key) fantastically effective, the political schmoozing of statesman-like scale and results are exhilarating, and his influence broadens and deepens inside and outside the business, political and development communities. He should get a medal. Oh, hold on – he did!

This is the whole story of how someone bold enough, smart enough, engaging enough turns society's dial. Goethe wrote, 'Whatever you can do, or dream you can, begin it.' Josh did. You could too. This book is a good place to start.

– Sir Bob Geldof
June 2023

Contents

Introduction

It was a balmy summer's day in Edinburgh, in August 2012, and the famous Edinburgh Festival Fringe had just started in the city. The Edinburgh Festival Fringe is the world's largest arts festival, and in 2012, it spanned 25 days and featured more than 55,000 performances of 3,548 different shows in 317 venues. The streets of Edinburgh were bustling with thousands of tourists enjoying all that the city had to offer.

Only two weeks earlier, I had co-founded and opened a small cafe in the centre of Edinburgh that we had called Social Bite, selling sandwiches and coffees to tourists and local office workers. I was only 25 years old, and this was my first proper attempt at running my own business, with all that entails – employing staff, making the food, coffees and serving the customers. We had rushed the launch so that we would be open in time for the Edinburgh Festival Fringe, hoping that the thousands of tourists descending on the city would get our brand-new business off to a good start.

Paying it Forward

On this particular day, while we were frantically making sandwiches and serving customers, trying to get to grips with our fledgling new business, a young man called Peter Hart wandered into our small cafe. Pete was a 19-year-old, outgoing young man, with a broad Scottish accent, a chipped front tooth and a glint in his eye. While his charming personality was disarming, you could tell from the brief exchanges we had with him that he had lived through too much hardship for his young years. Pete was homeless, and had been earning a living selling the *Big Issue* magazine on the corner near the front door of the cafe. I had passed Pete most days over the past two weeks on my way to open up the cafe, and I would occasionally pop out to bring him a sandwich or a cup of coffee. But this day, Pete wandered into the cafe and began to linger next to the counter, his *Big Issue* magazines tucked under his arm as he looked nervously at his shoes. I suddenly realised that Pete had been plucking up the courage to ask me for a job.

I was motivated by the idea that our little business might be able to make a difference, and giving this young man a job seemed like a good way to make an impact in our community. *What the hell?* I thought. We could use an extra pair of hands in the kitchen and having a job with a steady income might make Pete's life much brighter, rather than standing in the cold selling the *Big Issue* every day. On that day, when I offered Pete a job, I thought that I was changing the course of his life, but the truth is that he was changing the course of mine. Pete inspired a social enterprise that would go on to help over a thousand people off the streets; create purpose-built villages for those without a home; raise over £25 million to fight homelessness all over the planet; influence public policy; and inspire Hollywood stars like George Clooney, Will Smith, Dame Helen Mirren and Leonardo DiCaprio to join the cause. Neither Peter nor I could have dreamed of the impact that his courage would have on my life, and the lives of others.

Over a ten-year period, I learned that I have enormous power in my hands to help the most marginalised people in our society, simply by using my entrepreneurial abilities. But I am just a young, averagely talented, average-looking, state-school educated sandwich shop owner from Scotland. If this is the level of change that I can help to create in less than a decade, then what would be possible if thousands more young people could be inspired to focus their creativity on tackling the issues that they care about? What if business leaders used their vast resources and ingenuity to solve society's most pressing social problems? What if we could relinquish the drive to create vast personal wealth and instead harness the power of entrepreneurial thinking and the free market to solve the problems of poverty, hunger, homelessness and climate change, helping not just ourselves, but all of society in the process?

Why the world needs you to be a social entrepreneur

I write this book at a time of an almost perfect storm of social challenges. The world has emerged from the Covid-19 pandemic and global and local inequality is out of control. Hundreds of millions of people are living in extreme poverty, exacerbated by the pandemic, while huge rewards go to those at the very top. During the pandemic, factors including a stock market boom helped by central banks pumping trillions of taxpayer dollars into financial markets, the monopolisation of the vaccine supply by big pharmaceutical companies, and the proliferation of technology usage has together helped to create one of the most significant transfers of wealth in the history of humankind. During the first two years of the pandemic, the world's ten richest people more than doubled their fortunes from $700 billion to $1.5 trillion at a rate of $15,000 per second, or $1.3 billion a day. Over the same two years, the incomes of 99 per cent of humanity fell and over 160 million more people were plunged into poverty. Billionaires' wealth has risen more since Covid-19 began than it has in the last 14 years. Last year, CNN reported that billionaires had added $5 trillion to their wealth since the pandemic began.

The result of all of this is that there are more billionaires now in the UK and globally than ever before, and their fortunes have grown to record levels over the course of the pandemic. Meanwhile, the world's poorest got even poorer. The world's richest 1 per cent now have more than twice as much wealth as 6.9 billion people combined.

The issue of homelessness is one of the clearest and most visible indicators that society is failing to address its social challenges. Many of us living in wealthy cities encounter on a daily basis people sleeping in doorways or begging for loose change as we walk down the street. Throughout the UK, over 271,000 people experienced homelessness in 2022. In the US, with its reputation as the richest country on earth, the number of people who are homeless there is now approaching levels last seen during the Great Depression in the 1930s.

The refugee crisis has reached levels exceeding any point in human history. According to the UN Refugee Agency, UNHCR, almost 80 million people worldwide, the majority of which are children, have been forced to flee their homes. In fact, an average of one person every two seconds is forcibly displaced. It feels that almost every week we see heartbreaking news reports of refugees having drowned near the UK's shores as dinghy boats, packed with desperate people, fail to make it across the Channel.

Human-caused climate change continues to wreak havoc across the world, with extreme weather events worsening year on year – from wildfires to severe flooding – and the human race is running out of time to keep global warming within limits that will avoid major catastrophe for future generations and loss of life as we know it. Scientists warn of a mass extinction event unless we change course.

So, what is going wrong? Why are markets failing so much of humankind and our planet? With technological innovation developing at a pace unimaginable only a generation ago and a record number of billionaires being minted each year, why are so many people being left behind?

The reason is straightforward. The free market was never *meant* to solve social problems; in many cases, it even exacerbates the issues we face. The ideology of capitalism has no real challenger and marches on unabated, with clear progress on many levels, but also leaving devastation in its wake. An obvious example is that economic growth has fuelled global warming. The mechanics of this inconvenient truth are straightforward: higher levels of economic activity tend to go hand in hand with additional energy use and consumption of natural resources.

Another example of capitalism exacerbating a social issue is that the technological boom in Silicon Valley and San Francisco has resulted in a mass influx of highly paid tech workers to the Bay Area, which has in turn led to the demand for housing to skyrocket, the cost of rent to inflate, and, subsequently, tens of thousands of people being unable to meet their increased rental costs for their homes. This has led to the perverse situation of the Bay Area having one of the worst homelessness rates per capita in the Western world, while also having the world's highest concentration of billionaires. When I visited San Francisco on a fundraising trip in 2019, I felt like I was in a dystopian nightmare: apologetically stepping around so many people who were homeless as I made my way up into luxurious skyscraper offices to meet with major tech companies.

Capitalism is a game: we can rewrite the rules

On a micro level, the other reason we have not, as a society, solved our most pressing social challenges is to do with how we define 'success' within our culture. Capitalism is a human-made system, a game that we human beings have created. What are the rules of this game and how do we define the winners and the losers? It's really simple. The golden rule of the capitalist game is: *success = money*. Accumulating wealth is the name of the game and money is the clear metric of success. We all want to be winners, so our entrepreneurs tend to focus creative energies on money-making endeavours rather than harnessing our skills to address social problems in our communities.

Clearly, there are millions of individuals who wake up every day and do jobs that serve their community, often at great personal cost. During the Covid-19 pandemic, thousands of doctors, nurses and hospital staff bravely worked in rapidly filling hospitals with a lack of PPE equipment, and helped the country through one of the worst health crises in history. In the UK, we clapped for them in the streets every week. They deserved to be commended as modern-day heroes. Thousands more people work in the charity sector, often voluntarily or proactively choosing a lower income in order to pursue a career helping a cause that they care passionately about. Teachers often choose to teach out of a sense of vocation; to help children find their way in the world. Social workers, overseas aid workers, disability support workers, the list goes on. Our country desperately needs these people's devotion to their jobs and commitment to helping others.

But in the world of business, it is difficult not to get sucked into the cultural vortex of *success = money*. Social media is awash with influencers flaunting new Ferraris, Louis Vuitton handbags, glamorous mansions and all that the material world has to offer, tantalising us with what we could have if we could only afford it. Many billions of pounds are invested by marketeers on convincing us that we are incomplete and that the accumulation of new material possessions is our route to happiness. Then we turn on the TV to watch *The Apprentice* or *Dragons' Den* (the US version of the show is known as *Shark Tank*) where the clear definition of business success is financial wealth. Even in education, economics textbooks in schools and universities teach this one-dimensional rule: that the role of business is to maximise profit. Gross Domestic Product (GDP) growth, measuring economic output, remains the primary measure of almost every nation's economic progress, regardless of the impact on people and planet. The stock market investment model inherently requires continual economic growth and ever-increasing profits in order to generate returns for investors. With these cultural influences, the vast majority of budding entrepreneurs naturally have a primary goal of maximising financial return.

I recently watched an episode of *Dragons' Den*, in which the entrepreneurs pitching for investment were:

1. A tech cheesemonger, aiming to sell artisan cheese to an online consumer
2. A hair extension training academy
3. An innovative dog-lead business
4. A business that aimed to radicalise the everyday key ring market
5. A new handbag company that printed extracts from an erotic novel into their bags.

I found it to be a really entertaining show. Each entrepreneur who pitched their idea was extremely passionate and had clearly devoted their entire working life to their business dream. The ideas were all innovative in their own way. Many had invested all of their personal money into trying to make their dream a reality and the Dragons battled each other gamely to offer investment finance in the businesses they felt could generate the strongest return.

But my key question is this: with the myriad of social challenges that we are facing – from homelessness, to the refugee crisis, to a mental health epidemic – do we really want the country's leading young business minds to be focused on developing erotic handbags? In the face of a climate emergency that threatens the very existence of our species, is it really a pressing priority to develop innovative dog leads or key rings? Yes, these businesses will generate employment opportunities and tax revenues, but we need our entrepreneurial thinkers to do so much more than that. Society desperately needs our entrepreneurial minds to be creating new and innovative business models that proactively address the social challenges that we face.

Shows like *Dragons' Den* and *The Apprentice* further cement the rules of the entrepreneurial game. Those who become rich are the winners; those who don't make it, the losers. This definition of success proliferates throughout our culture, in the business world, through schools and universities. The end result is that almost every single entrepreneur's creative focus is on activities that are motivated by maximising profit and a financial return. Everyone in the business world gets so busy trying to win the game that we don't stop to remember that we can rewrite the rules.

When one-in-five entrepreneurs are social entrepreneurs

Please don't get me wrong, I love entrepreneurship. This is not a criticism of entrepreneurs, it's a love letter. Almost all of my close friends are entrepreneurs; my dad is an entrepreneur; the people I go to the pub with are entrepreneurs. They think outside the box, they are passionate, dynamic change-makers; they create employment, tax revenue and innovation. I have the deepest respect for any entrepreneur because I know what it takes to start and build a business of any kind. It can be unfathomably challenging. As Elon Musk, founder of Tesla and SpaceX, puts it, 'Running a start-up is like chewing glass and staring into the abyss. After a while, you stop staring, but the glass chewing never ends.'

My experience of being an entrepreneur is that your business can consume every thought in your head: every waking minute can be spent building your business. Then when you sleep, it will occupy your dreams. It requires a bloody-minded, singular focus to move mountains, overcome challenges and realise your vision. It demands immense sacrifice, oftentimes requiring you to prioritise your business over your family, friends and relationships. It can be a life-defining journey of overcoming the odds to make your dream a reality and achieving what you set your mind to.

This leads to the core of my argument – my call to arms. If more entrepreneurs turned their mountain-moving work ethic towards solving our social problems, then our social problems would, indeed, be solved. I am not saying the entire business world needs to be turned on its head; things wouldn't even have to change too much. I believe that if only one in five entrepreneurs in our country created a business that relinquished the personal profit motive in order to focus single-mindedly on solving our social problems, we would make major inroads as a society to resolving these issues. If one in five investors, like those on *Dragons' Den*, sought out ideas that could make radical inroads into our social challenges and backed them with significant financial resources, then we could accelerate the rate of social change like never before.

Imagine a country where issues such as homelessness and child poverty were eliminated and everyone had enough to live a happy, fulfilling life. I believe we could achieve this as a society, and achieve it fairly easily. But only if we have enough focus on it. Only if we are not all too busy trying to win a game that we should be rewriting the rules of.

A social enterprise is a business set up with the sole focus of solving a particular social problem. To illustrate my point, in the UK today, there are currently an estimated 99,000 social enterprises with employees. This compares to 1.4 million private sector businesses with employees. Put simply, fewer than 1 per cent of the enterprises created in the UK are exclusively socially motivated enterprises, compared to 99 per cent private sector companies with a more traditional private profit motive. My call to action is for us to create a society that encourages a 20 per cent share of enterprises to be focused on solving our most pressing social challenges.

To help play this theory out, imagine the following hypothetical scenario of how society may evolve. At the start of 2021, there were 5.5 million small businesses (with 0 to 49 employees) in the UK making up 99.2 per cent of the total business activity in the country. Small and medium-sized enterprises (SMEs) accounted for three-fifths of the employment and around half of turnover in the UK private sector. Total employment in SMEs was 16.3 million people, while turnover was estimated at £2.3 trillion. If we could create an evolution in our society where 20 per cent of business activity was delivered through social enterprises, then we could harness annually an estimated £460 billion of privately generated revenue to help solve the pressing social challenges that we face. We could capitalise on the creation of roughly 3.3 million job roles to provide employment opportunities for marginalised groups who may be otherwise excluded from the traditional employment market. Most importantly, we would have over 1.1 million entrepreneurs using their creativity, work ethic and business ingenuity to create products and services that solve the key challenges in their communities that they are passionate about. That means 1.1 million of the country's entrepreneurial thinkers getting out of bed every morning and focusing their energy on innovative solutions to issues such as poverty, homelessness, the mental health epidemic, the cost of living crisis and climate change. This collective entrepreneurial energy directed towards our social challenges would create an unstoppable army of change-makers, with self-propelling business models that could accelerate the pace of social change to a level that is simply unattainable by slow-moving government institutions.

How could we create such a shift? It would require a significant movement in our cultural norms and how we define success within our society. It would require the education system, from primary school onwards, to inspire young people to change the world and give them the tools to do so. I had never even heard of the term 'social enterprise' until long after I had left university, but we need to teach social entrepreneurship to children as a career path. It would require top business schools to motivate and equip at least 20 per cent of their graduates to create world-changing social enterprises. It would require us to fundamentally shift the cultural rules of the game; to redefine success and start celebrating those who have delivered the most social impact through their entrepreneurial endeavours.

Many entrepreneurs become 'serial entrepreneurs' who create multiple businesses to bring a range of their ideas to life. If you are a serial entrepreneur and you go on to create multiple companies, why not create one of them as a social enterprise – with a mission to tackle an issue you care about? You can still achieve all of your personal financial goals through your traditional companies, but at the same time you can express your altruistic motivations through the creation of a social enterprise that will be single-minded in its focus to address a social challenge. If you are so inclined, you can have the best of both worlds by creating a traditional commercial business and a social enterprise!

Alongside traditional metrics like turnover and profit, business KPIs for a social enterprise would be focused on areas such as:

- the number of people helped out of poverty
- the number of employment chances created for those otherwise excluded
- meals distributed for the hungry
- the amount of carbon removed from the atmosphere as a result of your innovation
- the amount of safe drinking water provided for those in need.

Cultural shifts that could foster a greater number of social entrepreneurs in society could include:

- new television shows where budding entrepreneurs pitched their social enterprise ideas for investment
- new books, new academic courses, new online resources and masterclasses
- dethroning Instagram influencers who flaunt their wealth, in favour of people who sacrificed themselves in order to create change in their communities
- the creation of a 'social stock exchange', in which a marketplace of ideas could create positive social and/or environmental impact, and secure investment
- inspiring the investor community to channel 20 per cent of its vast resources towards business propositions that will bring about the most significant social change, even if it means a lower economic return.

Paying it Forward

The power of entrepreneurial energy

How long would it take the human race to solve major issues like homelessness, the refugee crisis or climate change, if 20 per cent of our entrepreneurial focus and financial resources were harnessed proactively in that direction? Looking at the unfathomable progress that the free market makes each generation, I don't believe that it would take very long at all.

For example, in January 2004, neither Facebook nor the iPhone existed. Within less than 20 years, less than one generation, 6.4 billion people – 78 per cent of the world's population – are now using smartphones. The majority of people on planet Earth, me included, are wandering around all day fixated on an illuminated glass handheld device which did not even exist at the turn of the century. Today, 4.55 billion people are using social media, 58 per cent of the global population. We are all now connected through social media in ways we could never have imagined two decades ago. The pace of change the free market creates is truly phenomenal. When entrepreneurial energy aligns with financial resources, it is a truly unstoppable force. It steamrolls a rate of change that a government could only ever dream of delivering. My argument is simply to harness a greater percentage of that unstoppable energy and direct it towards creating a world without poverty; where our planet is protected for future generations. Given that entrepreneurial icons like Richard Branson, Elon Musk and Jeff Bezos are now privately flying to space, my guess is that if we had a stronger entrepreneurial focus on solving planet Earth's problems, we could fix many of them within a generation.

Introduction

What about the role of government?

You may take the view that it is not business's responsibility to solve social challenges and that is the role of government. Businesses pay taxes, while governments are surely meant to represent the interests of society at large. However, if we are to rely on government alone, the challenges we face will simply never be solved. There are various reasons for the inefficacy of the public sector in solving our challenges. These include the short-term nature of the political cycle, which does not incentivise the solving of long-term problems that might take more than four years in which to make inroads. Furthermore, politicians are often more concerned with saying and doing things to stay in power, which means focusing on policies that benefit their target voters rather than on the problems that affect already marginalised groups.

Another central issue is the often terminally slow and bureaucratic decision-making structures that are endemic in public institutions, which can have the effect of suffocating the kind of fast-paced and dynamic environment that thrives in the private sector and is often necessary to create change. Governments by nature are notoriously slow, inefficient, bureaucratic and often ineffective. Combine these structural issues with the all-too-prevalent incompetence of the political class, and it means that we cannot simply leave it to the politicians. You only had to turn on the news during the height of the Covid-19 pandemic to see the incompetence and at times downright corruption (when awarding multi-million-pound contracts to cronies and insiders) of the current UK government.

The rate of change that occurs when entrepreneurship is aligned with financial resources is on a different plane to what the public sector can deliver. It's easy to think that by paying our taxes and voting in an election, we have discharged our duties as citizens and it's over to the politicians to represent society's interests. But we cannot be so passive. If we wish to create change in the world we have to take the power into our own hands. In the words often attributed to Mahatma Gandhi, 'Be the change you wish to see.'

What about the role of philanthropy?

The father of modern philanthropy was Andrew Carnegie (1835–1919). Carnegie was among the wealthiest and most famous industrialists of his day. By the age of 30, Carnegie had amassed business interests in ironworks, steamers on the Great Lakes, railroads and oil wells. He was subsequently involved in steel production and built the Carnegie Steel Corporation into the largest steel-manufacturing company in the world, becoming the richest man on the planet at the time.

Carnegie believed in giving wealth away during one's lifetime, one of his most famous quotes being, 'The man who dies rich, thus dies disgraced.' Through the Carnegie Corporation of New York, the philanthropic foundation he established in 1911, his fortune has since funded libraries and paid for thousands of church organs in the United States and around the world. Carnegie's wealth helped to establish numerous colleges, schools, non-profit organisations and associations in his adopted country and many others.

Carnegie's life has become the foundation of the traditional philanthropic model: entrepreneurs focus the main thrust of their working lives on their business activities, thereby amassing wealth. Then, after achieving great riches, they choose to give money away to support charitable causes in the latter half of their lives.

Introduction

In more recent times, global philanthropy has been advanced by the 'The Giving Pledge', a campaign created by Bill and Melinda Gates and Warren Buffett, to encourage extremely wealthy people to contribute the majority of their wealth to philanthropic causes in their own lifetime. As of June 2022, the pledge has 236 signatories from billionaires based in 28 countries.

Philanthropy makes a phenomenal difference in the world. My own charitable organisation Social Bite has received countless amazing contributions from incredibly generous philanthropists that have helped to aid our work in tackling homelessness.

Philanthropy is a critical part of civic life and part of the life-blood of the charity sector. But the Carnegie philanthropic model has not managed to make a dent in many of the social ills that we face. Indeed, at a time of record levels of wealth and philanthropic giving, many of the social challenges we face have got significantly worse. The problem is that what the world *primarily* needs is not these individuals' charitable donations. The world needs to harness their entrepreneurial creativity and ingenuity, their drive and determination, the attributes that made them so successful in the first place. In the current system, the vast majority of entrepreneurs are giving the best of themselves to the pursuit of that wealth. The majority of their creative energy, their innovative thinking and their world-beating work ethic is focused on building their private businesses. Philanthropy comes second. It has to, by definition: you have to make the money in order to give it away. Philanthropy typically happens at the tail end of an entrepreneur's career, when they are in the autumn of their lives. I wonder what many of the great entrepreneurial minds could achieve if they applied their creativity towards developing new and exciting business models to solve our social ills? I believe the difference they could make would be exponentially greater than what can be achieved through traditional philanthropy. With this new way forward, we could begin to truly address the social challenges the world faces.

What's in it for you?

We have a myriad of problems to face: the potential impending demise of our species through climate change, the exponential cost of living crisis, and the societal challenges that confront us every day as we walk down the street or turn on the news. But why else should you consider devoting yourself towards becoming a social entrepreneur? What's in it for you? Why should you be the one to relinquish personal profit, while others are working hard to make money for themselves?

Firstly, it's fun. It makes life interesting. You meet a range of weird and wonderful people that you would never otherwise meet and create life experiences that you would have never dreamed possible. Over a ten-year period, during my twenties, I had experiences that included living in a one-bedroom flat with three people who were homeless for two years; interviewing President Bill Clinton live on stage in front of 2,000 people; taking Hollywood megastars George Clooney and Leonardo DiCaprio to Scotland for a sandwich; building a village for people who were homeless to live; shutting down Times Square in New York for a 'sleep out'; and raising over £20 million for a cause I am passionate about. Over the last decade, I have grown as a leader and as a human being, making hundreds of mistakes and seeking to learn from each one. These

Introduction

are just a handful of experiences from many I could share, and not a single one would have happened had I not proactively chosen to relinquish the motivation of achieving significant personal wealth, instead making the decision to put people over profit.

Secondly, you live a life of purpose. You get out of bed each day, knowing that your working day is going to be filled with meaning. In the UK, the US and much of the Western world, we live in a society that has more wealth, prosperity and technological advancement than at any time in human history.

Yet at the same time, death rates from suicide and addiction are also at record highs. Why? We are experiencing a crisis of purpose in Western society. We are being sold a lie that making money will provide our lives with the meaning we crave. It never can: at a profound level, living a life with purpose is what most of us yearn for, beyond any material gain. Helping others is the key to finding happiness.

In 2013, my own personal hero, Nobel laureate Muhammad Yunus, took the stage at the second annual Forbes 400 Summit in front of some of the richest people in the world and gave a speech. 'Making money is a happiness. And that's a great incentive,' he told the attendees over dinner in the United Nations Delegates Dining Room. 'Making other people happy is a super-happiness.'

In this book, I will share with you the entrepreneurial journey I have taken so far. Each chapter will focus on a particular lesson I have learned over the last decade and will offer you advice as you set out on your own path to change the world, in your own way. As I share my story, I will conclude each chapter by offering the key things I believe can help and inspire you in your own mission.

Paying it Forward

I do this in the hope that you will join me in devoting your entrepreneurial creativity towards helping the people and the causes that need you most. The world needs you to embark on your own exciting path of social entrepreneurship in order to help others. By doing so, I hope you will find a 'super-happiness' for yourself.

Chapter 1
What is social entrepreneurship?

I call myself a social entrepreneur, but what exactly does this mean? The dictionary definition of entrepreneur is, 'a person who sets up a business or businesses, taking on financial risks in the hope of profit'.

I have an alternative definition of entrepreneurship, which is not related to the pursuit of profit per se. To me, entrepreneurship is simply the act of bringing an idea or vision from your mind into reality. The act of creation. Another word for this is 'manifesting', a term particularly utilised in today's social media age. Stephen R Covey said that 'all things are created twice'.

Everything around us was first created in someone's mind, before being brought into reality. The chair that you're sitting in, the bus you took home, the television you watch tonight, the screen or paper upon which you are reading this book; literally everything around you was first conceived as an idea in someone's mind. Then there was a process to bring that idea to life, which likely involved a lot of blood, sweat and tears and, ultimately, the successful execution of a business. This process of bringing something from your mind into reality is thrilling. I love it. I'm addicted to it. I launched my first business when I was 21 years old and it lit a fire within me that has burned bright ever since. I still get the same buzz any time I manage to bring an idea from my head into the world.

Depending on what your idea is, you may have to overcome all kinds of hurdles in order to bring it to reality. You might need to secure finance. You will likely have to employ people with the skills you need and galvanise them around your vision. You might create manufacturing capability, or distribution infrastructure, or have to hit the road and sell your product or service to your potential customers. Every day will bring a new set of challenges and that never stops. But, if successful, you will reach a moment when one day the vision you had in your head plays out in the real world. The creation happens twice. When that happens, you realise that the world is in fact malleable. We all have the power to influence and change it. One of the world's most famous entrepreneurs, Steve Jobs the founder of Apple, sums up how I would define entrepreneurship in this quote:

When you grow up, you tend to get told that the world is the way it is. And your life is just to live your life and try to not bash into the walls too much. But that is a very limited life. Life can be much broader, when you discover one simple fact. And that is that everything around you that you call life was made up by people that are no smarter than you. And you can change it. You can influence it. You can build your own things that other people can use.

Shake off this erroneous notion that life is just there and you are just going to live in it, versus embrace it, change it, make your mark upon it. When you learn that, you will never be the same again.

So, for me entrepreneurship is simply the process of bringing an idea into the world and making it a reality. This is a skill and the more you practise it, the better you get at it. The entrepreneurial process, by nature, involves routinely taking risks and living with uncertainty. It requires you to be entirely self-motivated and to be comfortable with having no prescribed structure. It is completely different from having a paid job where you will have a specific remit, secure income and a boss providing instruction and guidance.

Are entrepreneurs born to this state of mind or can it be taught? I don't know the answer, but I do feel that an entrepreneurial life is more naturally suited to certain people. Entrepreneurs tend to be outliers and oddballs. People who don't mind taking the path less trodden and aren't afraid to think differently. Common characteristics of entrepreneurs tend to be those with a higher appetite for risk, an ability to sell their vision to others and a desire to be their own boss. Entrepreneurs are those who are able to translate their vision into reality, usually in the form of successful businesses.

Social entrepreneurship

If entrepreneurship is simply the process of bringing an idea from your head into reality, then social entrepreneurship is directing this process towards a particular social challenge. Put simply, it's having an idea of how a social problem can be solved and translating that vision into reality. To do so, you will need to overcome all of the same challenges as a traditional entrepreneur. You might need to secure finance, to employ and motivate people, to manufacture a product and to sell your idea to your customers or donors. But the motivation that gets you out of bed each morning is driven by a cause rather than the prospect of personal gain. It is putting purpose first over profit.

Coming out of the Covid-19 pandemic, we find ourselves in the eye of a perfect storm of social challenges. Unfortunately, a social entrepreneur is spoilt for choice: homelessness, the refugee crisis, climate change, loneliness, suicide, mental health, addiction, race relations, unemployment, knife crime, cost of living. The list could go on and on. The act of social entrepreneurship involves having an idea to tackle one of these pressing challenges and bringing it to life.

There are various models that social entrepreneurs can pursue. I am not an advocate for any particular model, the key thing for me is for entrepreneurs to use all of their creative energies to tackle the social problem and this can be done in many different ways. The foundation, for me, is to be cause-driven rather than profit-driven. Here are the key models a social entrepreneur can bring to life:

1. Starting a social enterprise

Social enterprises are businesses that are designed to sustainably tackle a social challenge. Like traditional businesses they aim to make a profit but the profits are reinvested or donated to create positive social change, rather than being taken out as dividends.

What is social entrepreneurship?

My social enterprise, Social Bite, is a chain of high street cafes. We compete with the likes of Starbucks and Pret a Manger. We sell sandwiches and coffees to customers, which generates the revenue to make the business sustainable. However, I do not own a single share in the business and nor does anyone else. We gave 100 per cent of the shares to a parent charity – an entity that has a sole purpose of reinvesting funds in helping to tackle homelessness. There is no private profit motive. Instead, the purpose of the business is to provide employment opportunities for people who were homeless and we run a 'Pay It Forward' service where customers can buy an extra sandwich or coffee that people who are homeless can pick up later. (Indeed, the idea of paying it forward is so central to our mission that this is the title of this book!) This helps us give out 140,000 items of food and hot drinks every year. One in four of our team are from a homeless background. We have branches in four cities, and last year we opened our first London cafe on the Strand.

Other well-known examples of social enterprises include the *Big Issue* or the Eden Project. There are over 100,000 social enterprises throughout the country contributing £60 billion to the economy and employing 2 million people.

Social Enterprise UK defines a social enterprise as a business that:

- has a clear social or environmental mission that is set out in its governing documents
- is an independent business and earns more than half of its income through trading
- is controlled or owned in the interests of the social mission

- reinvests or gives away at least half of its profits or surpluses towards its social purpose
- is transparent about how it operates and the impact that it has.

Critically, social enterprise differs from *charity* because it is funded through selling a product or service rather than through donations. This can make the project inherently sustainable and also opens up opportunities to scale the enterprise through attracting social investment.

Social business model

My own social enterprise journey was inspired by a Nobel Peace Prize-winning economist, Professor Muhammad Yunus. Professor Yunus pioneered the concept of 'social business', which has a narrower focus than the social enterprise model outlined above. Yunus describes a 'social business' as a 'non-loss, non-dividend company that exists exclusively to address a social challenge'. The company should cover all of its costs and generate a profit, while addressing a social cause. The impact of the business on people or the environment, rather than the amount of profit made in a given period, measures the success of social business and no investor or founder should ever take dividends from the business, so all profits are reinvested in expanding the impact. This model differs from the social enterprise model detailed above because it advocates that the social business is profitable and self-sustaining through trading, whereas the social enterprise structure only advocates that more than 50 per cent of its income is derived from trading. This means that the social business model adopts stricter commercial principles, whereas the social enterprise structure is better suited to a hybrid model that can be part-funded through donation income, alongside trading income.

Earning a living and equitable salary structures

When I first set up a social enterprise and gave 100 per cent of the shares in the business to a parent charity, I asked myself the question of how I would earn a living. I wanted to focus my creative energies on helping our most vulnerable people, but like anyone else, I wanted to sustain myself. I had the same aspirations as most others, in that I wanted to be able to get a mortgage, have enough money to travel and hopefully take care of a family one day. As our social enterprise grew, I also wanted to be able to hire experienced people, and knew we would have to pay a higher salary level to attract them.

We decided to implement a policy that the person at the top of the leadership hierarchy should earn a fair salary, but their remuneration should never be more than seven times the salary of the person at the bottom level of the organisation, which was a metric recommended to me by Muhammad Yunus at a social business conference that I attended. If your organisation pays the living wage to all of your employees then this leaves plenty of room for your own earning potential as well as room to attract talent to your organisation. To put this policy into perspective, let's look at the pay disparity in the private sector, which has accelerated over the last six decades. In 1965, CEOs in the US earned 15 times more than the average worker, but by 2015 it had risen to 351 times. In the UK in 2019, the bosses of FTSE 100 companies were earning

117 times the salary of their average worker. That means it would take over 100 years for the average employee at one of these companies to earn what their CEO makes in one year.

I find that the policy we have implemented strikes a balance that enables me to earn a good living from my work, but turns off the greed impulse of focusing my effort on becoming extremely wealthy and accumulating more than I need. Instead, with a fair salary in place, I am able to focus my creative energies on maximising the social impact I am able to create. It also enables the company to attract talent to senior positions within the organisation, where being able to offer competitive salaries is important.

Another example of an equitable salary structure proving to be a big success was when, in 2015, Dan Price, the boss of a card payments company in Seattle called Gravity Payments, introduced a $70,000 minimum salary for all of his 120 staff – and Dan personally took a pay cut of $1 million to pay for it. Five years later he is still on that lower salary and says the gamble has paid off.

In an interview with the BBC, Dan Price said: 'People are starving or being laid off or being taken advantage of, so that somebody can have a penthouse at the top of a tower in New York with gold chairs. We're glorifying greed all the time as a society, in our culture. And, you know, the Forbes list is the worst example – "Bill Gates has passed Jeff Bezos as the richest man." Who cares!?'

What were the results of this unusual decision by Dan Price? The headcount of Gravity Payments has doubled and the value of payments that the company processes has gone from $3.8 billion a year to $10.2 billion. But he is prouder of other metrics. In that same interview he said, 'Before the $70,000 minimum wage, we were having between zero and two babies born per year among the team, and since the announcement – and it's been only about four and a half years – we've had more than 40 babies.'

2. Social investment

Social investment is the use of finance to achieve a social as well as a financial return. Money is provided by investors who want to see it paid back and see that it has been spent on making society better.

Social investment provides finance to build an organisation's long-term capacity to achieve its social mission. It is not an income source, but a financial tool that can create opportunities for social enterprises to scale up.

Social investors often offer better interest rates and more flexible terms than high street lenders as they are looking for social returns as well as financial. 'Social returns' are metrics directly related to the impact the enterprise is seeking to deliver. These returns will vary depending on the focus of the social enterprise and could range from meals distributed to people in poverty, to helping people who are homeless into housing, to carbon emissions removed from the atmosphere as a result of a new innovation. Social investors are more likely to be willing to accept higher levels of risk and lower levels of financial return in exchange for social impact.

Social investment can help by providing working capital or by enabling social enterprises to create new ways of delivering goods and services, such as buying a building or investing in equipment or staff.

To be able to utilise social investment, a social entrepreneur will need to create a business model that generates a profit in order to pay back the investment with a reasonable rate of interest. Creating a model like this has the potential to achieve significant scale in tackling the issue you care about and the rate of growth of the organisation can be accelerated.

3. Founding a charity

The most traditional way you may seek to create a social impact is by founding a charity. Your charity will have a specific focus on a particular social challenge and you will devise services that will make a difference to the people you are trying to help. Your funding will largely be sought through securing donations, where the public, philanthropists or businesses can make donations to your organisation to help you achieve your goals.

While Social Bite started life as a social enterprise, we also registered a parent charity. We have undertaken a range of ambitious projects to tackle homelessness, which have been supported by generous donations rather than through trading. These projects include building a village for people who are homeless, which houses 20 people at one time in a community environment, a nationwide housing programme to help almost 1,000 people off the streets and a global fundraising campaign where 60,000 people 'slept out' in the freezing cold to raise funds all over the world. These activities fall more within the domain of traditional charity rather than social enterprise.

If you wish to fundraise and raise donations as part of your venture then you will realistically have no other options but to create a charitable entity. In Chapter 6, I detail some of the challenges for social entrepreneurs in setting up charitable entities, where the founder may have to relinquish some strategic ownership and adhere to a governance structure which places ultimate decision-making responsibility in the hands of a separate board of trustees. As an entrepreneur, this structure can bring its own challenges, so I would encourage all founders to consider the pros and cons when setting up a charitable entity.

4. A hybrid model

My own experience has shown me that it doesn't make sense to be too rigid in your model. Creating a social enterprise business model is a really exciting process, where you have to creatively try and marry the challenges of selling a product or service to your target customers to generate an income, while delivering a social impact. This can be the most sustainable and scalable way of tackling a social issue and can also open up possibilities of attracting social investment finance. However, this is not mutually exclusive with also operating a charity. You may wish to bring some projects to life by raising donations to support your idea and many of the things we have achieved to tackle homelessness would not have happened without generous charitable donations.

So, my advice is don't be confined by a particular model. Just get out there and start using your creativity to make a difference. Have fun and see where the road takes you!

Chapter 2

The cards we are dealt can define our destinies

So, how does one become a social entrepreneur in the first place? It's certainly a question I get asked a lot. I can only speak to my own experiences and hope that they resonate with others. Therefore, in order to answer that question, it's best to start at the beginning, so I will tell you a bit about my childhood and the things that shaped my journey later in life.

Given that I have spent almost all of my working life developing an organisation to help people who are homeless, I am often asked if I have a background of homelessness or poverty myself. In fact, I grew up in what I would consider to be a position of relative privilege. Looking back, I feel extremely lucky. I had a loving upbringing and was given the support and encouragement to create a life I wanted to lead. As I grew older, my childhood experiences became a motivating factor for me in trying to tackle the inequalities I encountered, as I began to meet many people who were homeless who were dealt vastly different cards from my own.

Paying it Forward

I was born on 16 September 1986, in a small village in central Scotland called Blair Drummond, the first son of Simon and Heather Littlejohn, with my only brother, Jack, following three and a half years later. Both my parents grew up far from wealth or privilege, my mum from a small farming community in the Highlands of Scotland and my dad from a working-class family in Chester in England, brought up by my staunchly socialist grandmother, Jennifer, and grandfather, Bill.

The year before I was born, my entrepreneurially spirited parents decided to take a gamble and open their own restaurant bearing their surname – Littlejohn's. They didn't have very much money at the time and had no funds to invest in interior decoration for their new venture. So, they emptied the garage of old bric-a-brac – bicycles, old car registrations, old clocks and anything they could find – to hang on the walls and create a unique decor for the restaurant. They had a small train track with a miniature train running around on the ceiling, had loud jazz music on the stereo and a well-priced, exciting menu. The restaurant was well ahead of its time in the eighties and pioneered the casual dining restaurant market in Scotland. It was a big hit with the locals in central Scotland and soon became a booming business.

As a child, my mum stayed at home to look after Jack and me. She was and remains an amazing, loving and supportive mother, and has been invested in every step of my life from childhood right until now, cheering me on and supporting me every step of the way. And, for as long as I can remember, my dad has been a big inspiration: he has always been an extremely hard worker, investing long hours in the business as he made it a big success, all with the motivation of providing me and my brother with every opportunity in life. He soon opened up a chain of Littlejohn's restaurants in other cities in Scotland and became well known as a prominent local businessman. As a family, we moved into a beautiful family home in Blair Drummond with a big driveway, acres of garden space complete with a large tree house built in one of the oak trees in the garden. It was a perfect family home for young children, with space to run around, a big living room with an open fire, and it even had a billiard room with a full-size snooker table!

My dad had aspirations to keep expanding the business and create a UK-wide restaurant chain. However, this changed when his father passed away suddenly from a heart attack aged only 58. My grandfather's sudden passing greatly affected my dad, especially as I was only two years old and my mother was pregnant with my brother, Jack. My dad decided that life was too short and he wanted to spend more time with his young family. He decided to sell the Littlejohn's restaurant business and sold up to a large company in a deal that made him and my mum millionaires before their thirtieth birthdays.

This meant that Jack and I grew up in relative privilege. We really had been dealt the best possible cards. Despite our family's wealth, my parents decided that my brother and I would not go to a private high school and we went to a local state school called McLaren High School in Callander. It was a great school, with pupils from all different kinds of socio-economic backgrounds. This was the first time in my life that I remember becoming aware that I was from a wealthy family, compared to most of the other teenagers at the school, and I hated that feeling. I became really embarrassed about being a 'rich kid' and tried to hide any sign that

Paying it Forward

I was from a wealthier family than anyone else. I was reluctant to invite friends round to my home in case they judged me for the house being too big. My dad drove a fancy sports car and I was mortified if he ever dropped me off at school. I used to make him park around the corner and then walk the remaining distance to school so that no one would see the car.

I began lashing out at my family's wealth. This translated into a sense of political idealism and led to a desire to 'change the world' in some way. I became angry and passionate about issues of inequality and poverty and started to develop an aspiration to do something about these things with my life. Jack and I started listening to Rage Against the Machine whose lyrics we used to yell at the top of our lungs in a passionate cry of naive rebellion.

Throughout our teenage years, we became increasingly politically engaged. We used to give my dad a hard time and say things like, 'Why is it fair that we should have this money when people are starving in Africa? You should give all of your money away to charity!' When a family friend fell on hard times and was struggling to pay her mortgage, we used to say to my mum and dad, 'That is not fair. You should pay her mortgage; we have more than enough.' Looking back, it was really unfair on my dad, as the main reason he wanted to make money in the first place was to take care of his family and provide my brother and me every opportunity in life. Furthermore, he had to work incredibly hard to do so. But as two idealistic and politically charged teenagers, we couldn't see that at all. We only saw our family's wealth as a symptom of an unfair economic system, under which some people thrived while others were downtrodden and excluded.

The cards we are dealt can define our destinies

This outlook undoubtedly helped to push me down a path of social entrepreneurship. If I have always felt uncomfortable and even slightly embarassed about wealth, why would I devote my career to chasing it? I never subscribed to the idea that money bought you happiness. I had encountered many very wealthy people in my childhood and none seemed particularly happy. In my career, I have met several billionaires, some of whom seem downright miserable. They have achieved wealth beyond their wildest dreams and realised that, after a certain level of income, it didn't actually alter their happiness.

Money can't buy happiness

My childhood intuition was confirmed when I learned that the idea that vast wealth leads to happiness has been disproved by science, at least up to a point. Experts say that happiness does increase with income, but the correlation peaks at earning the equivalent of $75,000 per year. 'The lower a person's annual income falls below that benchmark, the unhappier he or she feels. But no matter how much more than $75,000 people make, they don't report any greater degree of happiness,' *Time* reported in 2010, citing a study from Princeton University conducted by economist Angus Deaton and psychologist Daniel Kahneman. I think that Del Boy, in the British sitcom *Only Fools and Horses*, had it spot on when, after finally achieving his dream of becoming a millionaire, he still wasn't happy: 'This time next year, we'll be billionaires,' he tells his brother, Rodney. This view is commonplace among the rich. The belief that more money will make you happier does not disappear even when you have a net worth of more than £1 million, according to researchers from Harvard.

Paying it Forward

Michael Norton, a professor at Harvard Business School, asked 2,000 millionaires how happy they were on a scale of one to ten and how much more money they would need to reach ten on that scale. 'Basically everyone says [they'd need] two or three times as much,' Professor Norton told the *Atlantic* magazine. He found that about a quarter of millionaires with a net worth of more than £1.18 million said that they would need eleven times more money to be perfectly happy, one quarter said they would need six times as much wealth and another quarter said they would need twice as much. This pattern 'did not differ by wealth' and the belief that they would need a lot more money to achieve perfect happiness was expressed even by those with a net worth of more than £7.5 million. Even at the highest levels of wealth, the desire to become richer does not disappear, according to Jeffrey Winters, a political science professor at Northwestern University. He said, 'Every billionaire I've spoken to, and I've spoken to quite a number of them, is extremely excited by each additional increment of money they make.'

Knowing these psychological realities, why would anyone want to subscribe to this hamster wheel definition of success? In this paradigm, even when you grasp wealth beyond your wildest dreams, happiness still slips through your fingers, like chasing a rainbow. Since I felt this in my gut from a young age, after high school I went to Edinburgh University to study politics and economics, with an ambition to embark on a career that would focus on living a meaningful life and might make a difference in the world in some small way.

Years later, when I founded Social Bite, I repeatedly heard the personal stories of people who have found themselves homeless and was struck by the stark contrast between their childhoods and my own. I heard time and again of the harrowing childhoods that the vast majority of people who end up on our streets have lived through. The number one causal factor of homelessness is not people making bad choices in their lives, as many of us assume, rather it is childhood poverty: being born into a situation over which they have no control or agency. Homelessness is invariably linked to children who have been through traumatic childhood experiences: who have suffered abuse, lived through severe poverty or grew up in the care system.

The more people I met who were homeless, the more it became apparent that the cards we are dealt can define our destinies far more than the decisions we make. I became aware that we are systemically failing vulnerable children, letting them fall through the cracks and ultimately allowing them to end up on the streets. As a society, we still have collective compassion for children who have suffered abuse or poverty. However, when that childhood trauma manifests in later life as mental health struggles, addiction or homelessness, society all too often turns its back.

I have been widely recognised for my work as a social entrepreneur, receiving an MBE from the Queen, multiple honorary doctorates, a Robert Burns Humanitarian Award and a Pride of Britain Award. But I know that there is no such thing as being 'self-made'. We are all unwittingly shaped by the circumstances we were born into and the toolkits we were afforded through love, support and financial help. The cards I have been dealt have undoubtedly shaped my path and given me the freedom, ability and support structures to pursue whatever path I chose. On the other hand, many of the people I met who were homeless were dealt the opposite cards when they came into this world, set off on a path of trauma, poverty and exclusion. It is them who deserve the awards and the recognition in our society: for surviving, for managing to stay on their feet and for working to put their lives on a positive path, despite having the most difficult start in life. There, but for the grace of God, go I.

The cards we are dealt can define our destinies

Lesson: Never have to work a day

To summarise, we are all inadvertently shaped by our childhoods, our upbringings and the tools we have been equipped with. If you understand the things from your past that have shaped your outlook and motivations in life, then you can harness these motivations to pursue a path that aligns with who you are as a person. By aligning your core identity with what you do for a living, you will never have to work a day in your life, as you will ultimately be pursuing what you are passionate about and you will be emotionally and intellectually fulfilled by your work. If you succeed in achieving all of your wildest aspirations, don't give yourself all of the credit and fall into the trap of thinking you are self-made. The cards you were dealt likely had as much to do with it as you did.

By the same token, the people you meet in your life have all been shaped by the cards they were dealt. So, when you see someone struggling, behaving badly or battling with issues such as addiction, mental health problems or homelessness, then remember that they may have suffered trauma, they may have been failed by society from a young age, and they may need a compassionate approach that recognises the burden they have had to carry for too long.

Putting it into practice

1. Acknowledge that everyone is born, raised and brought up into a situation that is never of their choosing. These are the cards that they have been dealt and is something that they cannot choose.

41

2. Be aware of your own privileges and the biases that you may have.

3. Learn that people can transcend the cards that they are dealt in order to better their circumstances and make the best choices for themselves and for others.

Chapter 3
Calculate risk (your way)

Booking President Bill Clinton

Any entrepreneur will tell you that, at one point or another, they have had to take a leap of faith. This is because they might be stuck in the same place, or because their enterprise is in danger of failing, or because they might be faced with many forks in the road and don't know which one is necessarily the best one to take. When you reach this position, you hope that you will land on your feet, although there is no certainty that you will.

I remember my first big leap of faith, which taught me so many lessons relating to risk-taking in entrepreneurship. The first juncture in my life where I decided to take a major risk came when I managed to book President Bill Clinton as the keynote speaker for an event I had created. As crazy as it sounds, I took this gamble when I was only 24 years old, three years after I had graduated from university.

Paying it Forward

Upon graduating from Edinburgh University with a degree in politics and economics, I still had a clear aspiration to have a meaningful career and create a purposeful life. My original ambition upon leaving university was that I wanted to become a civil servant and work for the government. My dreams included working as a development economist advising poor countries how to grow their economies or going to work for the United Nations.

With this ambition in mind, I applied for a graduate job with the UK government as an economist. It was a six-month-long 'grad scheme' interview process where you had to do various psychometric tests that took place over days in assessment centres in London, as well as many other hoops and hurdles to jump through and over before being offered a job. After this six-month-long process, I simply received an email with a single sentence: 'We are very sorry, you have been unsuccessful in your job application.' I became disillusioned with this kind of interview process and didn't want to have to jump through all those hoops again just to be told I wasn't good enough. So I decided maybe I could follow in my dad's footsteps by setting up my own business and trying to create my own destiny. My parents had always taught me that 'you can achieve anything you set your mind to', so I thought I would put that to the test.

At the time, as with most of society, my own personal definition of a successful entrepreneur was defined in financial terms. Indeed, this was drilled into me during my study of economics at university, where I was taught that the mission of a business is to one-dimensionally maximise profits, and that is the role of an entrepreneur. While I wasn't motivated by becoming personally wealthy, when I decided to create a business, I signed up to the rules of the game and I wanted to win. *Success = maximising profits.*

I ideated different business concepts and most of them seemed to revolve around organising events, so I decided to set up my own events company which I called Capital Events – largely with the objective of creating profitable events to make some money.

My parents had separated by this time, and after university I was back living with my mum in our old family home. I started the events company from my old childhood bedroom where I brain-stormed different event ideas. Many days I would be making phone calls and sending emails from my bed. The first event that I dreamed up was a fashion show I decided to organise to coincide with the Edinburgh Festival that I called 'The Festival Fashion Show'. Looking back now, I was 21 at the time, single, and I thought that organising a fashion show could be a good way to find myself a girlfriend! I booked a venue in Edinburgh and gave myself a few months to pull it all together. I approached high street retailers like Karen Millen and Debenhams to ask them to exhibit new clothing ranges for my show and managed to recruit models, secure sponsors and sell tickets. In the end, I created a great event which sold 300 tickets, I had a great time and I made £3,000. I thought, *Wow, this entrepreneurship thing is amazing!* I was buzzing! It felt like a light had switched on within me, where for the first time I realised that you could have an idea in your head and work to bring it to reality. It was an addictive feeling and I was hooked.

I started renting a small office in the centre of Edinburgh and started to dream up more ambitious events. I began to create exhibitions. The first was called 'Scotland's Christmas Fair', where I booked out the Royal Concert Halls in Glasgow on the weekend before Christmas and charged Christmas gift companies to come and exhibit and sell gifts to the public on this busy weekend. From this event, I ended up making a profit of £20,000. I thought I had the Midas touch! I can't deny that it was a real thrill to create an event and earn a chunk of money from my idea. I felt like a true entrepreneur. The next exhibition event was more ambitious still – an event I created called 'Scotland's Ski and Snowboard Show'. For this event, I took a big risk and signed a contract to book out the SECC – Scotland's largest exhibition and conference venue – for a cost of £40,000. I then embarked upon selling exhibition stands to snow sports companies and created a big marketing campaign to sell thousands of tickets for the public. Most snow sports companies I spoke to were not particularly interested so this was a crash course in learning how to sell. The options were to sell for my life or go bankrupt! I managed to scrape by in the first year, losing money and being extremely close to going under. I remember things got so tight that I was in the office one day phoning around insolvency hotlines for advice. I was able to get a bridging loan from the bank and survived by the skin of my teeth. Having learned valuable lessons, I then repeated the event the following year and managed to make £50,000 profit.

I was developing a real flair for entrepreneurship and wanted to keep upping the ante. I had realised that if you put the word 'Scotland's' in front of an event name it sounded like a big, credible, national event so I decided to keep going with that formula and I created a business awards ceremony called the 'Scottish Business

Awards'. By this stage I had recruited a small team working from the office and we embarked on creating the nation's largest and most prestigious business awards ceremony. It didn't matter that we were aiming to create this from thin air: *fake it until you make it* was the philosophy.

I decided to try to recruit a judging panel of prestigious business leaders to judge the awards. I managed to persuade Duncan Bannatyne, who at the time was one of the 'Dragons' on the TV show *Dragons' Den,* to be the chairperson of the judging panel. I created 12 different awards categories such as 'Entrepreneur of the Year', 'Employer of the Year' and 'Green Business of the Year'. I then researched and wrote a letter to many companies and successful business leaders in Scotland informing them that they had been nominated for a particular award. Because we framed the event as the national and pre-eminent business awards ceremony, people receiving the letters assumed it had been around for many years and was very prestigious – and of course we didn't correct them! We managed to get all of the 'great and the good' Scottish business leaders there on the night: Sir Tom Hunter, Sir Tom Farmer, Sir Ian Wood, Jim McColl OBE.

People would often ask me how on earth I managed to get all of these top business figures in the room on the first year of the event and my answer was simple: we nominated them all for an award and they all showed up! We ended up with over 800 people attending the ceremony in year one and we booked Sir Bob Geldof as the keynote speaker. The night was a great success.

The following year I decided to try and secure an even bigger speaker to give the keynote address at the dinner, and although it might seem an unrealistic leap, I decided to try and bring President Bill Clinton to Scotland for the dinner. President Clinton clearly would have much wisdom to share, having presided over the longest period of peacetime economic expansion in American history. He also ran a global philanthropy initiative so I thought it would be an unbelievable coup to have him as a speaker at our Scottish Business Awards dinner and that he could help me make it the biggest event of its kind in the country.

I'm not sure what possessed me to believe that this was possible. I had absolutely no connection with President Clinton so I started very simply by googling his name! I found the Clinton Foundation's website and clicked on the 'Contact' page. It was one of those pages where there wasn't even a phone number or an email address, only a 'contact box' to fill out. I thought, *Here goes nothing*, and typed in details of our business awards event and enquired about President Clinton becoming the speaker. I hit send and assumed nothing more would realistically come from it. To my surprise I got an email from a representative at the Clinton Foundation asking some questions about the event. After some back and forth I decided to ask outright, 'What will it take to bring President Clinton to Scotland to be our speaker?' She replied that realistically we would need to make a 'very substantial donation' to the Clinton Foundation for him to make the trip. When I asked 'how much?' I was told we would need to make a donation of at least $210,000 to make it happen.

At the time, I had almost no money in the bank, but that didn't deter me. I did a few sums and I figured that with Clinton's name attached, I could sell a certain number of tables at the dinner at a price of between £2,000 and £3,000 per table. I calculated that I could just about cover the $210,000 donation if I was successful in selling enough tables. So, thinking that you only live once, I reached back out to my contact at the Clinton Foundation and said, 'Let's go for it!' She then said, 'Well, it's not quite as simple as that. We can't just give you President Clinton's name to advertise as we don't really know who you are! If you want to book him you need to pay the donation in instalments. So, we would need the first $60,000 within two weeks of signing the contract, a further $60,000 after one month and the remainder prior to the event.' *Oh, God*, I thought, not sure what to do. It would be a massive gamble and I had no idea if I stood any chance of raising the funds required, particularly in those tight timescales. I remember sitting in my tiny office with the contract in front of me and a pen in my hand, thinking it over.

My exact thought process was something along the lines of *Fuck it!* I signed the contract and posted it back. It was a massive gamble but something in me told me I could make it happen. I had two weeks to raise the first $60,000 instalment.

I started to think, *Who do I know that I can sell a table to?* I frantically phoned anyone who had attended the dinner the previous year and explained it all to them. I had booked President Bill Clinton to speak and I needed them to buy a table from me quickly to raise the funds required to make the donation to his foundation. Enough people said, 'Wow – President Clinton! Count me in!' and bought a table there and then and arranged immediate payment. I managed to make all the donation instalments to the Clinton Foundation, and President Clinton came to Scotland in June 2013, where I interviewed him on stage in front of almost 2,000 business leaders. This was fairly daunting for someone in their early twenties!

The first thing I asked him was to tell us about his thoughts on the Scottish Independence debate (knowing that Alex Salmond and Nicola Sturgeon were in attendance) and I also asked, 'What's next for Hillary?', as everyone was wondering whether she was planning to run for president at the time. I absolutely loved the experience and I was buzzing with the process of being able to come up with a pretty far-fetched idea and manifest it into reality.

When I was sitting there interviewing President Clinton I knew right there that this world is malleable. We each have the power to influence and change things and bring our own visions to life. It was like my dad had always told me: 'You can achieve anything you set your mind to,' and I was starting to understand that there were no limits to that.

*

What this experience really opened my eyes to was how amazing things can happen when you relinquish the personal profit motive. At this particular time in my life, I was not motivated by making money for myself. I had kind of 'switched off' the personal profit button in my mind as a motivator and 'switched on' the buttons rewarding new life experiences and making an impact. If I had been primarily motivated by maximising a financial return for myself, there would have been no way I would have signed the contract for a $210,000 donation to the Clinton Foundation. It would have made absolutely no sense to commit to such a significant cost. I would have been way too focused on trying to ensure that most of the profit from the dinner would make its way into my own pocket. But by turning that button off, it enabled me to make a more unusual decision. This decision ultimately paid off and turned the dinner into a major annual event.

Through the Scottish Business Awards, we went on to bring other world-leading figures to Scotland to speak at this dinner, including Sir Richard Branson, George Clooney and Leonardo DiCaprio. With me organising the event every year, alongside my good friend Alan Mahon, the Scottish Business Awards attracted over 2,000 people annually and became by far the largest business dinner in the UK. It also went on to become a major fundraiser for our subsequent work in tackling homelessness.

My journey as a social entrepreneur had begun.

Lesson: Calculate risk (your way)

This experience of booking President Clinton taught me an important lesson about taking risks.

If you want to embark on a career in entrepreneurship, social or otherwise, you will need to get comfortable with taking risks. While the risk I took with President Clinton was a major risk, the truth is that an entrepreneurial path has risks and uncertainty at every turn.

Putting it into practice

1. *Balance value against risk*

To calculate the risk for you, my first piece of advice is to ask yourself two questions.

    a. What do you value in your life?

    b. What is the worst-case scenario if your risk does not pay off?

At this time, my answer to question one was that I valued trying to create a life with purpose, packed with new life experiences. I passionately did *not* want to be confined to an unfulfilling nine-to-five job that didn't give my life meaning or provide me any excitement, variety or purpose. My answer to question two was that the worst-case scenario if my risk did not pay off was that, at the very start of my career, I would be sued by President Bill Clinton! Now *that* would be a pretty interesting life experience! It would be something I could tell my grandkids about at the very least (or write about in a chapter of a future book)! So, my decision to sign the contract made complete sense, because of how I framed the risk in my mind and what I perceived as the downside.

If you are leaving education and trying to figure out your path in life, or are in a nine-to-five job that is not bringing you happiness, then you need to consider the 'risk' of taking the conventionally safe option. By taking the safe option, you could be risking a lifetime of not being fulfilled through your work. You could look back on your life and wonder what could have been. To me, that is the biggest risk of all. If you decide to embark on any kind of entrepreneurial path, sometimes you may have to put all of your chips on the table. So, ask yourself what it is that you most value and what is the worst-case scenario? If the balance is right on your own mental scales, I would encourage you to take the leap of faith. You never know how it might change your life.

2. Work out to whom and for what you are accountable

The second key thing to learn from this experience is to take risks when you are relatively free of responsibility and accountability for others. At this time in my life, I had no major responsibilities, no big mortgage, no children or family to support. It's much easier to take the gamble and put all of your chips on the table when you are young and have fewer responsibilities.

A few years ago, I met a beautiful woman named Sukhi and I fell head over heels in love with her. Finding a love like I have found with Sukhi has undoubtedly changed my outlook and priorities in life. I have become less work-focused and have embraced other joys in life, like travelling, creating new experiences and spending quality time with family and friends. In late 2021, I became the luckiest man alive: we got married, and we have recently bought a flat together. When I started to write this book, I found out the amazing news that Sukhi was pregnant with our first child and baby Theodore has now recently arrived!

At this juncture in my life, would I take the same financial risk I did then? Hell no, I wouldn't! Like all of us, as I grow older, my priorities are changing. My personal values and worst-case scenarios have evolved with age as my life has changed. When you are weighing up what you value vs the worst-case scenario, that calculation is likely to change as you get older, because life brings more responsibilities and you start to value other things.

3. Know that you can influence the odds in your favour

The third lesson from this moment in my life relates to the nature of gambling in an entrepreneurial context. If I were to empty out my bank account, go into a casino and put all of my money on the colour black on the roulette wheel, my odds would be roughly 50 per cent to win and double my money, or 50 per cent to lose everything. In a casino, when your chips are placed on the table and the wheel starts spinning, you have no control over the outcome – your fate is with the gods of luck. Whereas in an entrepreneurial context, gambling is very different.

When I decided to book President Clinton to speak at my event, my metaphorical chips were certainly all on the table. At the very moment that I took that decision and signed the contract for $210,000, my odds of pulling it off were probably less than 50 per cent – the odds were not in my favour. But the amazing thing about risk-taking in an entrepreneurial setting is that, unlike a casino where it is all down

Calculate risk (your way)

to chance, you can spend every waking minute influencing the odds in your favour. Every time I picked up the phone and sold a table at my event to help me fulfil the contract, my odds got a little bit better. Day by day the probability that your gamble will succeed gets stronger and stronger until you become a red-hot favourite and eventually you make sure that your gamble pays off. Of course, sometimes your gamble will not pay off and you will make a mistake in your decision. In fact, you will make hundreds of mistakes throughout your entrepreneurial career. But while you will make hundreds of mistakes, you will also make thousands of decisions. Learn from each mistake and you will ultimately achieve your goals.

Chapter 4
Find your inspiration

Meeting Professor Muhammad Yunus

In the words of Isaac Newton, 'If I have seen further than others, it is by standing upon the shoulders of giants.' When embarking on your own journey of social entrepreneurship, it is important to find people who can inspire you and help shape your path. Is there someone in your community you look up to who is trailblazing social change? Perhaps there is a global figure leading the way in tackling the issue you are passionate about? Indeed, I hope that by sharing my own journey in this book, you can take inspiration from my own experiences. While you will need to carve out your own path, there are all kinds of lessons and inspiration you can take from people who have gone before you.

I found my inspiration in a Nobel Peace Prize-winning social entrepreneur named Professor Muhammad Yunus. It was mid-2011 and I had spent the last three years building my events company.

Paying it Forward

I had managed to create a range of events that I was really proud of and I was in the midst of planning my first Scottish Business Awards event, described in the previous chapter. By this stage, I was completely addicted to the buzz of entrepreneurship. I loved being able to have an idea, work really hard and see it come to life. Despite my new-found passion for entrepreneurship, I was starting to feel increasingly hollow because nothing I was doing aligned with the ambition I had dreamed of since my teenage years: of making a difference in the world. As much as I was loving bringing my increasingly ambitious ideas to life, I was feeling a bit empty. I felt myself starting to grasp for ways to make my life more meaningful and more connected with the burning idealism that I used to have when I was younger.

Around this time, I stumbled across a copy of Muhammad Yunus's book called *Creating a World Without Poverty: Social Business and the Future of Capitalism* and it changed the course of my life. Professor Yunus is an incredible man based in Bangladesh who won the Nobel Peace Prize in 2006. He is best known for founding an organisation called the Grameen Bank, which offered loans to poor rural women in Bangladesh in order for them to start their own micro businesses. Professor Yunus is the founding father of what has become known as 'microfinance', a poverty reduction tool which has been used through-out the world to help millions of poor women gain access to funding, in order to create businesses and work their way out of poverty. Many of the women Professor Yunus lends money to cannot read or write (and therefore cannot sign contracts) and who have never had access to finance before. Grameen Bank now lends more than $1 billion per year to over 10 million women who would otherwise have no access to loan finance. These women have now been able to create their own businesses and earn an income for themselves and their families, breaking the cycle of poverty.

In his book, Professor Yunus described an idea that he calls a 'social business'. He described how in his native Bangladesh, he had created over 50 different companies, some of which went on to become billion-dollar businesses. But here's the difference: he never owned a single share in any one of them. The motivation for him was never the traditional one of maximising profit for himself or for shareholders. He did not subscribe to the idea of business and entrepreneurship that I had learned in economics, watched on *The Apprentice*, or read in a traditional business book, where success was defined by accumulating wealth. Professor Yunus created businesses because he witnessed a myriad of social problems in Bangladesh and his solution was always to tackle these challenges through business solutions.

Professor Yunus's book perfectly combined my new-found passion for entrepreneurship with my long-held motivation to help people and make a difference. I thought, *Wow, this is the idea for me!* I had been searching for more meaning in my life and this was something I could grab on to with both hands.

Inspired by his ideas, I decided to reach out to Professor Yunus and see if I could come to Bangladesh and meet him. Looking back this seems a bit rash and impulsive, but some sense of inner purpose was compelling me and I felt that this was my path. I suppose I took my own advice on balancing risk and taking a leap of faith. I wrote to Professor Yunus in Bangladesh to request a meeting. When I didn't hear back, I persistently phoned his office and eventually got through to his assistant. After phoning consistently for several weeks, probably just to stop me pestering them, his assistant even-tually said, 'He will be in Bangladesh in October. If you can come all the way here, then you can meet him then.' 'Book me in!' I said.

I booked for me and my partner at the time, Alice – who was working with me in my events company and later became the co-founder of Social Bite – to go to Bangladesh in October 2011. We spent one week in Bangladesh, during which time we met Professor Yunus. We had been to a local clothes shop in Dhaka and we turned up to the meeting wearing full Bangladeshi garb. I have since learned that everyone thought it was hilarious that I arrived looking like some kind of 'Latter Day prophet'. We visited a branch of Grameen Bank and met rural women who were borrowing microloans to invest in creating their own businesses. We travelled to see Professor Yunus's other social businesses, including an eye care hospital for the poor and a business called Grameen Danone, which was producing yoghurt fortified with vitamins and nutrients for malnourished chil-dren. We travelled to remote areas of Bangladesh where no one had seen white people before; we were mobbed by local people who were all keen to meet us and shake our hands as though we were famous superstars, just because we were white.

It was a crazy, inspiring and unforgettable experience and one that would alter the course of my life. I invited Professor Yunus to visit me in Scotland and speak at an event, addressing Scotland's business leaders with his vision for a new form of capitalism.

This experience lit a fire in me and I was determined to come back to Scotland to create our very own 'social business'. I decided to sell off the bulk of my events business for £50,000 and invest it in this mission. Social Bite was born.

Find your inspiration

Lesson: Find your inspiration

Social Bite would not have happened without me finding a hero or a mentor to inspire me, or without having the persistence and confidence to reach out to them. Pushing myself out of my comfort zone to travel to Bangladesh and immerse myself in the work of Muhammad Yunus gave me the inspiration to commit myself to a completely different path in life.

Sometimes it can be too easy to follow the path of least resistance in life and stick to the track we are on just because we have found ourselves there. My advice is that if you feel a deeper sense of calling, then do everything you can to align what you do for a living with who you are as a person. If you manage to align those two things, you will be unstoppable.

Putting it into practice

1. Find your inspiration

Just like I found Professor Yunus to inspire me, if you are planning to embark on your own social enterprise journey, then I would encourage you to find someone or something to give you inspiration; someone who can help you think differently and take a path less followed. I often think if I hadn't stumbled across Professor Yunus and his work, I might never have lit the fire that was within me.

Whether your inspiration comes from a Nobel Peace Prize winner, someone in your community, or an author or a leader in the field you wish to enter, be sure to seek out inspiration to inform your journey and light a fire within you.

2. Reach out to your heroes

The other takeaway from my story is to not be afraid to reach out to the people who inspire you. Muhammad Yunus offered me advice, inspiration and later even travelled to Scotland at my invitation. You never know unless you try.

3. Identify mentors who resonate with you

Think about your values and the areas you are really passionate about pursuing. There will almost certainly be many people who have gone before you that have helped to pave the way in the area you want to work in. So I would advise you to do your research, read lots of books on the things you are passionate about and find the people you can learn from and be inspired by. The best mentors resonate with something inside of you and can help you unlock it and bring it into the world.

Chapter 5
Find your purpose

The creation of Social Bite

The origins of any new venture or social enterprise will usually start with a brainstorming session. My co-founder, Alice, and I had been inspired by Muhammad Yunus to set up our very own social business, but we didn't know what kind of business we wanted to create. So we started to bash ideas around what kind of business format would make a difference in our community? At the time I had a small office in the centre of Edinburgh for my events company and most days I would go out and buy a sandwich from Pret a Manger or a coffee from Starbucks. We thought that if we could create a cafe that sold great coffee and sandwiches, but one with a social mission, then possibly customers would choose our cafe over the more corporate chains. So, we settled on the idea of opening a cafe with a social mission. The original idea did not have anything to do with the homeless issue, instead the concept was to try and make a profit and we had selected different charities to donate the profits to. We then considered names for the business. The original name that we landed on was 'Social Sandwich', but when our friend Lucy suggested the name 'Social Bite' during a ideation session, we thought it had a ring to it, and it stuck.

In your journey, there will come a point when you may think you have done all the planning you need to do. You know which social issue you want to address, you know your proposed business model and you are ready to launch your social enterprise or charity. As my story will show, don't be too wedded to your original plan and try to be flexible and pivot to address the needs you encounter. You will have to dive in with both feet, but don't be afraid to swim in a different direction after you've got started in order to find your purpose.

We opened the first Social Bite cafe in August 2012. Inspired by our trip to Bangladesh, we wanted the business to have a social mission, but initially it didn't actually have anything to do with the homelessness issue.

We had found a cafe site in central Edinburgh on a popular street called Rose Street. It was just off the main shopping thoroughfare, around the corner from the same Starbucks, Pret a Manger and many takeaway coffee and lunch outlets that I used to frequent every day from my office. As I said, the original idea was to offer top quality food and coffee at a competitive price, hopefully make a profit – and then donate 100 per cent of our profits to various charities. We had selected three charities – two of which were international and one was local – to donate to. I had invested every penny of the £50,000 I made from selling off the bulk of my events business into the shop fit. To save money, Alice, my brother Jack and I painted and tiled the shop ourselves. We recruited a small team of staff, devised a menu of takeaway sandwiches, baguettes and salads, and got ready for opening day.

On the day we opened the cafe, we had literally run out of money in the bank – everything had been spent on the shop fit and the equipment. The fruit and veg supplier arrived with our produce order that morning and he expected cash on delivery. I had to make up some excuse and asked him to leave the fruit and veg and come back the following day for the money – hoping to pay him with the cash taken on opening day. So, to say we were naive and underprepared would be an understatement. We had never operated a food business before, clearly had no clue about cash flow management, and had no experience of managing a team. Looking back, I can only put it down to a series of small miracles that enabled us to survive as a business.

All logic would state that we should have gone bankrupt many times over – but through good fortune or divine intervention, we managed to survive and eventually thrive.

Each day we were in the cafe from 5am to 11pm making the food, serving the customers, cashing up the tills and then doing the prep for the next morning. The hospitality business is a gruelling one and we were exhausted, stressed out and learning everything as we went along.

After two weeks of the shop being open, the course of my life and the focus of our enterprise changed forever when a young man called Peter Hart came in one day to ask me for a job. Pete was homeless. I had met him a few weeks beforehand as he was selling the *Big Issue* on the street corner outside the front door of the cafe.

Paying it Forward

We used to say hello to him on the street and occasionally we would pop out with a coffee or a sandwich for him. On this particular day, Pete came into the shop and was awkwardly lingering next to the counter. I wasn't sure what he was doing, as he seemed to be hanging around by the till for about ten minutes, but in hindsight I realised he was plucking up the courage. 'Josh . . . erm . . . I was just wondering if it might be possible . . . maybe . . . if I might be able to get a job?' he asked nervously.

I thought about it for a while. *What might customers think if they see this young guy who was homeless in the kitchen?* I asked myself. *Will he be reliable? Can we afford another wage?* And then it struck me – this is meant to be a *social* business. The only reason we are here is to make a social impact. What better social impact could we make than offering this young guy a job? I couldn't really think of a better way to make a difference, so I said to Pete, 'You're hired; you can start in the kitchen tomorrow.'

Pete started with us as a kitchen porter, washing dishes, on a part-time contract for 16 hours per week. Even though most people would consider this to be a menial job, Pete relished it. He valued and appreciated the job so much that he wanted to work for his contracted 16 hours and then volunteer for another 16 hours on top. To him, it wasn't just a job. It was coming in out of the cold, literally and figuratively. It was losing the stigma of 'being homeless' and becoming part of a society. It was, for the first time, having colleagues and developing friendships at work. It was routine. It was purpose. It was a pay packet.

When you think about the millions of entry-level jobs that exist in the market, I often wonder why more employers don't open up opportunities to people who are homeless or excluded. In the current post-Covid, post-Brexit recruitment market, where employers are desperately trying to fill vacancies, there remains an untapped well of talented people who are traditionally excluded from the labour market. While doing so comes with its own challenges, as I will explain in the coming chapters, you can also find people who will value the employment so much that they will show a remarkable amount of dedication, motivation and commitment. Not only can you transform people's lives, but they can genuinely become some of your best employees.

When a full-time job became available, Pete was working so hard that it was the obvious decision for us to offer him a promotion. When another job became available, we thought, *Let's try it again*, and I asked Pete if he knew anybody else that was homeless that might want a job. He replied, 'My brother Joe is also homeless, also selling the *Big Issue*; he would love a job.' So, we decided to offer Joe a job too. Pete and Joe had grown up in the care system together and became homeless in their late teenage years. After a time travelling to Southampton to doing odd jobs and paving driveways, they returned to Edinburgh where they found themselves homeless. Joe also relished the opportunity of employment, seeing it as a chance to alter his path in life. He hit the ground running and excelled working in the kitchen on the food prep and cooking duties. Another job opened up so we thought, *Let's try it again!* and we asked the brothers if they knew anybody else from the homeless community. They suggested a man called John who was in his late thirties and who also sold the *Big Issue* magazine in town. Before we knew it, John was also employed in the cafe. At this point, I think it dawned on Pete, Joe and John that we were fairly sympathetic employers and they could help other people who were homeless to get jobs, so they started to recommend others. They suggested we take on a man called Colin who had been homeless for 15 years and was in recent recovery from a heroin addiction. A few weeks later Colin was also employed in our cafe.

Our approach to employing people from vulnerable backgrounds, much like everything else we were doing, was very naive. There was no training programme in place, no resources to support them in employment and we had no experience at all in working with vulnerable people. We just put them all in different jobs, treated them like human beings and learned as we went along how to make it work.

Things were thrown into chaos after several months when Pete and Joe's accommodation fell through. They hadn't told us about it, but we started to wonder what had happened when they were turning up to work obviously unshowered and unkempt. That wasn't really sustainable in a food business where hygiene standards are obviously very important, so I enquired with them what had happened. They explained that they had been staying with their birth parents after reuniting with them on Facebook but that this had fallen through and they had found themselves without a roof over their heads again. As with many people who are homeless, this meant that they would sometimes be on the streets, if not sofa surfing or in homeless shelters. We were faced with a difficult decision. Because of hygiene regulations for food businesses, it wasn't really feasible for them to continue working for us given their current living situation. But it would have been terribly unfair to make them lose their jobs just because they had lost a safe place to live through no fault of their own.

I had a small one-bedroom duplex flat in Stockbridge in Edinburgh where Alice and I lived, with a small living room upstairs. After talking it over, we decided to let Pete and Joe stay in our flat, sleeping on a sofa each in the living room. Professional boundaries clearly didn't form part of the thinking! We suggested we would accommodate this arrangement for a maximum of two weeks until we could sort something else out. Twelve months later, Pete and Joe were still living in my one-bedroom flat! Not only that – Colin had now moved in too! The flat was chaos, with the living room often a complete mess and bodies strewn everywhere as we squeezed into this small flat. Whenever one of the guys was late for work, having slept in, I would find myself walking back to the flat and buzzing the doorbell until they woke up to come to work. This living situation, alongside the pressures of running a small business, was extremely stressful and consumed all areas of my life. I put on three stone in weight. I think I was eating more to help cope with the stress and pressure and had no time to even think about exercise or hobbies that might form part of a balanced life. I was also always surrounded by sandwiches, which of course didn't help!

Looking back, the decision to commit to this organisation and these individuals in such a way may seem extreme. But at the time it seemed like the only obvious decision to make. We had absolutely no financial resources to utilise in order to support any employees who were homeless. If a situation arose like this where their accommodation fell through, I had to use whatever was at my disposal to make it work. In this case that meant sharing our living space. In the process, I developed deep bonds with these early employees as they taught me about the issue of homelessness, shared their personal journeys with me and their own spirit of resilience inspired me to keep going. The relationships I developed with all of the early guys that we employed – Pete, Joe, Colin, Sonny and many others – will, I hope, be lifelong friendships and many of them have gone on to become inspiring speakers on the issue of homelessness to this day.

*

As we got increasingly engaged in the issue of homelessness, we decided to try to expand our impact and we introduced a service in the cafe called 'Pay It Forward'. When customers were coming in to buy a coffee or a sandwich for themselves, we encouraged them to buy something else 'in advance' for someone who was homeless to get something for free later. Customers started to engage with this idea and bought extra soups, sandwiches, hot meals and coffees for people who were homeless to come in and redeem. We would charge the customer for the item, print off the receipt and put it in a big glass jar on the counter. We then put a handwritten sign on the window that said, 'Attention . . . We now run a "Pay It Forward" system. You are welcome to come in and get a free item of food and a hot drink. One item per person per day. Love from Social Bite'. Word travelled quickly around Edinburgh and people started to come in throughout the day – they would rummage through the big glass jar, pick a receipt and claim a sandwich or coffee for free. Before we had even realised it, we were feeding around 40 or 50 people who needed it every day in our small cafe. Between this free food provision and offering the employment opportunities to people who were homeless we had found the purpose of Social Bite. This would become the model of what would go on to become a nationwide chain of cafes throughout Scotland and London, competing on the high street with the major players like Pret a Manger, Starbucks and Greggs.

After 12 months of trading, we had employed various people with backgrounds of homelessness and had met a wide array of people on a daily basis coming in for free food. I became curious about the root causes of homelessness so I started to ask people their stories – 'If you don't mind telling me, how did you become homeless?' I would tentatively enquire. I must admit that I had some preconceived ideas about the issue of homelessness and how people might find themselves in that situation. Like many others I had some assumptions that people ended up homeless either through getting addicted to alcohol or drugs, or by making some bad life decisions. However, when I started to ask people about their journeys it started to become a bit spooky. No matter how many people I asked, day after day, I kept hearing an almost identical story repeated back to me. People would invariably tell me a version of a story with very similar parallels: they had typically suffered very traumatic childhoods, often being abused either physically, sexually or emotionally; they had often grown up in the care system, a system that failed them after they lived in various children's homes and foster homes; they had become homeless in their late teenage years and society turned its back – 'it's their own fault' was the mantra.

Paying it Forward

When I kept hearing broadly the same story on repeat, it became immediately obvious to me that homelessness was not a problem born out of individual decision making. It was *systemic*. People who were dealt certain cards when they came into the world were being failed systemically and almost funnelled into this desperate situation of homelessness and poverty. It seemed like some kind of perverse destiny. They had not chosen the world they would be born into any more than I had. The difference is that they were dealt the opposite cards to someone like me and society simply did not intervene properly to help catch them along the way. Furthermore, when they found themselves in the most vulnerable situation that most of us could imagine – homeless and alone – society cruelly stigmatised them and assumed it was their own fault.

There is undoubtedly a link between homelessness and addiction to drugs or alcohol, but the causal relationship is often the reverse of what people assume. More often than not, the addiction follows the homelessness rather than the other way around. Common sense will tell you the reason why. Imagine if you were homeless and living out a winter on the streets of a major city in the UK. Cold, unsheltered, unprotected and scared. How long would it take you to turn to some kind of escape through drugs or alcohol? I am sure for most of us, it would be no time at all. The more stories I heard from people talking about their homelessness, the more motivated I became to work to make a bigger difference.

So, by the end of our first year, we had truly found our purpose and our mission: to tackle homelessness and to create employment chances for those who would otherwise be excluded. We found that purpose, sometimes through trial and error, sometimes through taking risks and sometimes through serendipity, but we always had an unshakeable commitment to helping people. We developed a deep commitment to combat homelessness and to leave our footprint for good in the world. In our case, it had taken Pete plucking up the courage to ask for a job to help us uncover and truly define our purpose. This just shows it always pays to be responsive to opportunities to help others when they come your way.

Lesson: Find your purpose

When we offered Pete a job in our cafe, it helped to define the purpose of our organisation, which became focused on helping homeless people through offering employment and providing food. Our journey also helps to illuminate the importance of the social enterprise business model, compared to a more traditional private sector commercial business model, when it comes to tackling social issues and enabling a different kind of decision making. Because our business had a singular focus of maximising a social impact, it enabled us to make some more unusual decisions and walk a path less trodden.

The reality was that when we started to offer jobs to people who were homeless, we knew that it would likely cost the business more money than if we had recruited from the regular labour market. We had to be patient and incur increased costs: going on a journey from homelessness into employment would inevitably mean that these workers could potentially be less productive and less reliable than other workers. We had to invest in providing support alongside the employment.

Furthermore, when we started to offer free food to people in need in the cafe, we knew that this would mean losing some paying customers who, as much as they might want to support the cause, in reality would choose to frequent one of our competitors rather than queue behind someone who has come in off the streets for their lunch. So, as a business we began to make decisions that were directly contrary to the commercial objectives of maximising profits. The social enterprise business model enabled us to make decisions that put purpose over profit and to maximise our impact, in a way that is very difficult to do in a private sector business where the ultimate responsibility is to maximise a return for the shareholders.

Putting it into practice

1. The hierarchy of needs

When I was thinking about pursuing life as a social entrepreneur I was thinking about how I could address human needs in the people I wanted to help, as well as my own needs. I found the famous 'hierarchy of needs' model proposed by American Abraham Maslow in his 1943 paper 'A Theory of Human Motivation' to be illuminating. The hierarchy of needs is a motivational theory in psychology comprising a five-tier model of human needs, often depicted as hierarchical levels within a pyramid.

From the bottom of the hierarchy upwards, the needs are: physiological; safety; belongingness and love; esteem; self-actualization. Needs lower down in the hierarchy must be satisfied before individuals can attend to needs higher up.

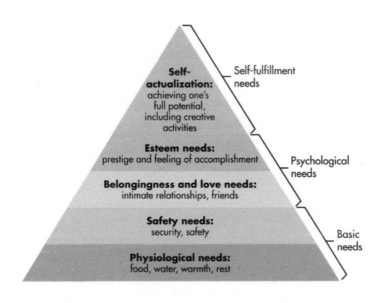

Maslow's hierarchy of needs is important when pursuing a career in social entrepreneurship for two important reasons.

Firstly, it further demonstrates the idea I have argued earlier in this book that pursuing vast wealth does not lead to happiness. As psychologist Daniel Kahneman found, 'no matter how much more than $75,000 people make, they don't report any greater degree of happiness.' Maslow's hierarchy illustrates that we each need a certain level of economic income to cover the first two levels on the pyramid – our basic needs of food, safety, home and security. Once these needs have been met, then money is effectively redundant in achieving the next three stages – love, belonging, esteem and self-actualisation. To paraphrase the Beatles, love can't be bought with money. I believe that the path of social entrepreneurship, and devoting one's working life to helping others, can better enable us to meet all of our needs identified on Maslow's hierarchy.

Secondly, when thinking about the kind of social enterprise or charity you want to create and how you might use your creativity to best help others, I would encourage you to focus your energy on the bottom two levels of Maslow's pyramid, where people do not have their basic needs met. By definition these are the most desperate people, most in need of your help. By seeking out those without access to food, water, warmth, security and safety we can make the biggest impact. For it is only by fulfilling these basic needs first that any of us can begin to overcome any other challenges in our lives.

2. Be prepared to pivot

The other key lesson I want to draw out for any budding social entrepreneurs from the creation of Social Bite is to not be too rigid

Find your purpose

in your plan and be prepared to pivot in your thinking. The purpose of Social Bite quickly evolved from when we first set up the cafe. We were flexible to pivot the orientation of our mission when Pete came and asked us for a job and we saw an opportunity to make a difference. The focus of our enterprise quickly shifted towards offering employment and food to people who were homeless as soon as we understood the need. If we had been too set in our original plan, we would have never established the right mission for the organisation. Sometimes you need to feel your way to the best destination after you have already jumped in. It may take some time to find your purpose, but it will feel right when you do.

Chapter 6
Personal sacrifices and challenges

Setting up a social enterprise can be the most rewarding thing you will ever do. But, I can't lie to you, it can also be one of the most stressful and mentally taxing things you might ever embark on, with a guaranteed roller coaster of emotions and challenges to contend with every day.

This chapter will focus on some of the personal sacrifices that you might have to make as a founder of a social enterprise or charity, and offer you advice on how you can personally deal with them. In this chapter, I also want to highlight the challenges you might encounter as a social entrepreneur if you choose to create a registered charity as the vehicle for your work, as opposed to a social enterprise or business structure that does not have to be a registered charity (please see Chapter 1 for an explanation of the different structures you may pursue).

Mental health challenges

Even though you will probably always be surrounded by others, being the founder of a charity or social enterprise can be lonely. You are no longer only responsible for yourself, but you will feel a responsibility for your employees, their families and the people you are supporting through your work. When you are offering employment opportunities to vulnerable people in particular then this can come with its own set of challenges, as if people lose their jobs, then this can plunge their lives into a crisis without a safety net.

As I outlined in the previous chapter, in the first year of Social Bite, my co-founder, Alice, and I moved three of our employees who were in a situation of homelessness – Pete, Joe and Colin – into my one-bedroom flat. We did this because their accommodation had fallen through and it would not have been right for them to lose their jobs just because through no fault of their own they had lost a safe place to live. We had no financial resources at our disposal to provide housing or support, so the only way to put a roof over their heads was to invite them to live in our small flat.

While we only planned to have them stay for a maximum of two weeks until we could find them alternative accommodation, all three lived with us for well over a year. This created a chaotic living environment, with five people squeezed into a one-bedroom flat. As I outlined in the previous chapter, this living situation, alongside the pressures of running a small business, consumed all areas of my life and without me realising it, started to affect my mental health. With no brain space for anything other than Social Bite, my lifestyle became unhealthy and I neglected my own physical and mental health, putting on three stone in weight without even noticing.

The pressure of this living situation led me to reach breaking point: I started to suffer from panic attacks. A panic attack is an intense feeling of fear or extreme panic that is brought on abruptly, often out of nowhere. These feelings of terror occur without warning and are disproportionate to any actual threat or danger. They are an evolutionary 'fight or flight' response that our ancestors developed when we were cavepeople and found ourselves faced with danger. An intense sense of panic would kick in and we would fight or escape, leading to our survival. But in the modern world, there are (for the most part) no life-threatening predators or natural disasters to contend with, so stress in our working or personal lives can instead trigger a disproportionate sense of panic and anxiety.

I would wake up in the night and find that my teeth would chatter uncontrollably and my whole body would tremble, and I would be hyperventilating with panic. I couldn't place where the sudden fear was coming from and I had never experienced anything like it, so at times I became convinced I was going to die. On multiple occasions, I ended up in A&E, where they would prescribe me Valium to calm me down. During the working day, I would be in the cafe serving customers and would feel physical symptoms build up very quickly: my heart was pounding and I started to feel faint, dizzy and light-headed. The all-consuming nature of setting up Social Bite – the financial pressure, the workload – and living in a one-bedroom flat with five people crammed in had put a severe strain on my mind and body.

Paying it Forward

What I have learned over the years is that in the early stages of setting up a new organisation, it is easy to be all-consumed by it. But it is really important that you work to establish a healthy balance in your life: there is much more to life than work and productivity. Furthermore, in order to best serve the organisation you have founded, it is critical that you take care of yourself. The stress of setting up our new social enterprise and everything that came with it had become too much for me to handle. I started to receive some Cognitive Behavioural Therapy (CBT) and mental health support at this time and managed to get on top of my anxiety and panic attacks. I took up running, got a gym membership, lost the weight and began to spend more time with my friends and family. Taking the time to get your mental health right, committing to regular exercise and establishing a more balanced life by seeing family and friends are all critical factors in your mental well-being. You can't help anyone else if you aren't taking care of yourself.

Financial challenges

It is likely that the biggest stress you will continue to encounter again and again as a social entrepreneur will be related to the financial health of your organisation. Most early stage enterprises will be cash-strapped and you will likely have to juggle paying suppliers, staff, rent and yourself in order to manage your cash flow.

In the early stages of the journey with Social Bite, I sold off one of my major events for £50,000 to invest in the shop fit. This left me with no personal savings and because the organisation's cash flow was so tight in the early years, I took almost no salary out of the business in order to keep as much cash in the bank account as possible. This inevitably led to me needing to juggle my own personal finances, falling into debt, frequently falling behind on my mortgage payments and ruining my personal credit rating for a long time. In the early days of Social Bite, I was doing so much juggling, I felt like I should join the circus! I hear many stories of social entrepreneurs effectively plunging themselves into poverty in the early stages of getting their idea off the ground. Many people do not see the sacrifice that goes on behind the scenes for founders as they commit to bringing their idea to life.

The challenge with founding any kind of organisation is that it will almost inevitably be cash-restricted in the beginning. This is because it is difficult to get financial backing and support without a strong business track record and evidence of success. It's not enough to just have a good idea. When your social enterprise is just an idea in your head, there is no proof of concept that you can demonstrate in order to secure financial support. Therefore, when first starting out and trying to get your venture off the ground, you will almost certainly have to put your money where your mouth is and invest your own funds and/or minimise any salary you are able to take from the organisation in the early years. You might also think of other creative ways to secure start-up capital, such as crowdfunding or securing social investment, but in the vast majority of cases, you will have to manage extremely limited financial resources to build your vision from scratch.

My advice to best navigate the financial stresses and pitfalls inherent in founding any organisation is to make sure that you understand the language of finance and accountancy. Many social entrepreneurs are deeply passionate about their cause and amazing at delivering the social impact, but all too often fall down due to a lack of financial knowledge and experience. Especially when you are managing very limited financial resources, it is critical that you teach yourself to understand budgets, cash flows, balance sheets and profit and loss accounts. It is only through careful financial management that your social business can survive those precarious early days and begin to thrive.

Management challenges

When founding a charity or social enterprise, you will undoubtedly need to go on a personal growth journey in your management style and how you lead others. How you go about managing people will need to evolve and change as your organisation grows.

In the early start-up stages of your organisation, your management approach will likely need to be more of a 'command and control' style. Your fledgling new venture will be very fragile and it is only you (and your co-founder, if you have one) who can protect it. Your cash flow is likely to be tight. Every decision could be make or break to the survival of your organisation. Clear and decisive leadership is fundamental to success. Achieving results is imperative. In the early stages, it's do or die. The reality of this start-up environment will likely lead to a management style that is very results-orientated. 'Softer' areas of leadership like team building, nurturing staff morale and facilitating people development will likely give way to a more urgent leadership style, focused on ensuring the job gets done. As you won't have much financial resource to employ lots of people, you will probably have to do many of the jobs yourself. When we first started Social Bite, the founders had to make the sandwiches, serve the customers, order the supplies, do the books, come up with the marketing strategy, raise the funding and be the HR department. There are never enough hours in the day, so buckle up.

Where it becomes more difficult is that, when the organisation grows and matures, your leadership style will have to change. The 'commander' style that made you the perfect leader in start-up phase will likely be the wrong leadership style when the organisation has matured and you have a larger team. Now that Social Bite is ten years old and employs around 70 people, the leadership required from me is very different to when we were just getting things off the ground. When you are running a larger organisation, your primary focus must be on recruiting amazing people who have the skills you don't, inspiring them to bring a vision to life. You can go much further through a collaborative approach than you can through the 'command and control' leadership approach that was so important in the early stages. Your focus will need to shift to ensuring your team are looked after, motivated and happy to keep working for your organisation. By contrast, in the start-up phase, it feels like more of a personal journey, but achieving a vision collectively should become the focus as an organisation matures.

These ever-changing leadership requirements will bring significant personal challenges to you as the founder of the organisation. As a founder, you may never have managed a team before in your life, so you should embrace that this is a growth journey for yourself. Listen to your team's feedback and adapt your style as your organisation grows. As soon as you are able to, recruit fantastic people to complement your own skills. Social entrepreneurship is definitely a team sport.

Challenges with the structure of a charity

In this section, I have outlined the significant personal challenges that you are likely to face as a social entrepreneur. You might have to invest considerable sums of your own money into the organisation; you might have to minimise your own salary to support the cash flow; you might find that your mental health takes a toll under the pressure, so you will have to continually take care of yourself and stay healthy; and you will have to continually evolve as a person and a leader.

The above is not just the case for social entrepreneurs; most entrepreneurs in the private sector will go through the exact same challenges that I have outlined here. However, the key difference for a traditional entrepreneur is that the structure of a private company will mean that they have a strong incentive in the form of a shareholding enabling them to benefit from profits generated by the business. Founders in the private sector also get to enjoy the perks of setting up their own business – such as more autonomy, being in control of their own destiny and being their own boss. These things tend to be the motivating factors as to why people set up their own businesses, in spite of the personal sacrifices involved.

As a social entrepreneur, if you choose to set up a registered charitable entity as the vehicle for your venture (which is really your best option if you wish to fundraise donations as part of your work), then the current legal governance requirement is that you must establish a board of trustees that, in many cases, could be made up of individuals who have no prior connection to you. Trustee board members will be unpaid volunteers and can often be amazing people that bring a lot of value and support to your organisation.

Clearly it is imperative that you find a like-minded group of trustees with a range of skill sets; people that you trust implicitly to govern the organisation you have invested so much of yourself in and sacrificed so much for. Fortunately, I enjoy a positive working relationship with Social Bite's chair and board members, some of whom have become close friends of mine. Our board of trustees also understands the unique dynamic of governing a founder-led organisation and harnessing that power alongside that of a talented wider team. If you are lucky enough to find great board members, then one of the central benefits is that the ideas you come up with will ultimately end up much improved by the time they reach fruition, after going through a process of rigorous scrutiny and guidance from board members. This is a process that I enjoy working through and it can be invaluable for delivery of projects.

But as a founder, you should be aware that, as your organisation evolves, the board will go through different life cycles, as each chairperson is entitled to populate the board with their own choice of people, who in many cases can be strangers to you. In the worst cases, this can lead to a difficult reality for far too many charity founders, where after putting in all the sacrifices, a group of non-connected board members can thank them for their time and ask them to leave the organisation saying, 'We'll take it from here'. This dynamic has happened to friends of mine and is more common than you might think within the charitable sector. Even if this eventuality does not arise, the personal autonomy and strategic ownership that founders in the private sector take for granted can be diminished for a social entrepreneur. You are no longer 'your own boss'; instead you can become effectively an employee, working for the board.

I understand the critical importance of checks, balances and oversight that a charity board structure creates. Clearly, in a context where donations have been made by the public, oversight, robust governance and a degree of collective decision making is important. I also know from personal experience the benefits a board structure can bring in helping to bring ideas to life in the best way possible. However, for me, existing charity structures can be very challenging from the perspective of incentivising founders to create charities in the first place and harnessing their driving energy to build the organisation and create social change. This ultimately results in fewer entrepreneurial leaders entering the charity sector at all.

Leadership within the charity sector, particularly larger charities, is absolutely dominated by 'professional charity CEOs' who climb the executive ladder within the sector and will jump from being the CEO of a homeless charity, to a children's charity, to a cancer charity and so on depending on the career opportunities that arise. Don't get me wrong, these professional CEOs can do a fantastic job of managing, leading and developing charities. However, their skill sets and ability to drive change are very different to that of entrepreneurs and founders who tend to have a very

Personal sacrifices and challenges

different approach. Think about some of the most successful companies in the private sector – Apple (Steve Jobs), Microsoft (Bill Gates), Facebook (Mark Zuckerberg), Tesla (Elon Musk), Virgin (Richard Branson), Huffington Post (Arianna Huffington) – they have almost all been led and driven forward by a founding entrepreneur. In the charity sector, it is extraordinarily rare to find a large, founder-led charity, because, in my view, the legal structure does not necessarily facilitate or support social entrepreneurship. Instead, many entrepreneurs gravitate towards a career in the commercial sector. Ultimately, I think that having fewer entrepreneurs encouraged to create organisations within the charitable sector is to the detriment of society and our ability to solve the social challenges that we face.

I personally believe that a new charity structure should be created and legislated for; one that delineates 'Social Entreprise' within the charitable ecosystem, and which can better foster a culture of social entrepreneurship. This new legal entity could be created in a way where oversight, checks, balances and robust governance are built into the model, and could also be regulated by existing charity regulators under new legislation. However, social entrepreneurs must be encouraged, supported and incentivised in a way that I don't believe they currently are within the existing legal structures that make up the charity sector.

The primary purpose of this book is to encourage people from all walks of life to make the required personal sacrifices and set up social enterprises and charities for causes that they care about. As I set out in Chapter 1 of this book, I believe that the only way we will systemically address the social challenges we face in society is through the proliferation of social entrepreneurship. It is critical therefore that entrepreneurs are supported and encouraged as part of the charity sector ecosystem and the appropriate legal structures exist to better enable a culture of social entrepreneurship.

Personal sacrifices and challenges

Lesson: Overcoming the personal challenges of a founder

Becoming a social entrepreneur and creating your own charity can be incredibly meaningful and rewarding, but go in with your eyes wide open; it is not easy. Make sure you are prepared for the personal challenges and sacrifices that lie ahead and equip yourself to overcome them.

Putting it into practice

1. Mental health

You can't take care of anyone else if you don't take care of yourself. Establish a work-life balance, spend time with friends and family and do other things outside of your new venture. It is easy for your new organisation to become all-consuming, but guard against this. Take the time to exercise and keep fit; it is so important for your mental health and you will perform better as a leader as a result. If your mental health cracks, like mine did, get help.

2. Financial health

Understand the language of finance and accountancy. While your passion to make a difference and achieve results will be your key driver, do not neglect financial literacy and careful financial management. Teach yourself to understand cash flows, balance sheets and profit and loss accounts. It is only through careful financial management that your social business can survive those precarious early days and begin to thrive. If you can, don't do what I did and screw up your personal credit rating by ducking and diving too much in the early days. It can take a long time to recover!

3. Management health

You will need to adopt an ever-changing leadership style. Your style at the start will need to be different as the organisation grows. Embrace this as a growth journey for yourself. Listen to your team's feedback and adapt your style as your organisation grows. As soon as you are able to, recruit fantastic people to complement your own skills.

4. Understand the challenges of a charity structure

There is currently no legal structure that a social enterprise fits into. If you wish to raise donations as part of your work, then your best option is to create a registered charity. Be aware of what this entails as the structural requirements can be challenging for a founder to operate within effectively. If you wish to join me in calling for the creation of a new charitable structure that delineates Social Enterprise as a structure and provides a supportive ecosystem for founders, while ensuring governance, oversight and safeguards are in place, then let's ask the government to create and legislate for this new type of entity.

I believe that this is important for facilitating the proliferation of social entrepreneurship that this book calls for. In any case, it is absolutely critical if you are to set up a charity as a founding entrepreneur that you take your time to find the right board of trustees who can help and support you and your team in delivering the mission in the best way possible, as I have been fortunate to find with Social Bite which has had many fantastic trustees over the last decade.

Chapter 7
Pray for miracles

When embarking on any entrepreneurial endeavour, you will need some luck. You will need to hope that the world conspires in your favour to help you overcome the daily challenges you will face and avert the many potential catastrophes waiting around each corner. When building an enterprise to tackle a social issue and undertaking the challenging work involved (such as, in Social Bite's case, employing people who are homeless and giving away 140,000 items of food each year in high street cafes), you'd better pray for miracles! In my experience, they will come. In the words of the 18th-century writer Horace Walpole, 'Serendipitous discoveries are made by chance. Found without looking for them but possible only through a sharp vision and sagacity. Be ready to see the unexpected and never indulgent with the apparently unexplainable.'

As Social Bite got more established in our work and we gained more experience in running the cafe, we decided to expand the shops and try to open a small chain of cafes. I used my Scottish Business Awards event with President Bill Clinton to put on a charity auction and we managed to raise the funds required to open more premises. Over the course of two and a half years, with funds raised at the Scottish Business Awards and the support of philanthropists like Sir Tom Hunter, John Watson OBE and the guidance of a board of trustees led by our chair, William Gorol, we expanded rapidly and opened up five cafes: two in Edinburgh, two in Glasgow and one in Aberdeen. We also opened a central production kitchen in Livingston where we began to produce the food centrally and invested in some vans to distribute the food to our shops. Gradually, as we grew from 2012 to 2014, we grew into a fairly sizable business, employing around 70 people. We made it a policy that a third of our staff would come from a background of homelessness. I recall the *Guardian* published a big feature piece with the headline: 'The homeless workers taking on Pret, Starbucks and Greggs.' We were the plucky underdogs, a workforce comprised of a cross-section of people who had been excluded and marginalised by society and were now taking on the system. As word spread around the homeless community about Social Bite, the demand for free food was increasing every day and we started to struggle to make ends meet financially. Our cash flow became tight and I started to worry we had grown too quickly, too soon.

We reached a crisis point when, after two years of trading, the big glass jars with the 'Pay It Forward' receipts were starting to run empty every day. The demand from people in need of free food was outstripping the amount of donations we were receiving from customers. We started to have to turn people away from the shops:

Pray for miracles

'Please come back later or try one of the other shops,' we would say, as people arrived in their droves to find the jars empty. Furthermore, the rapid expansion of our business had started to see it crack at the seams. We had no funds to support the considerable number of vulnerable people we were employing and many were struggling to maintain the structure of employment without some additional support. People we were employing from homeless backgrounds didn't have basic things like bank accounts. Most had never seen things like an employment contract. Many were used to living chaotically and struggled to adjust to the daily routine of a job. These challenges meant that many of our employees who were homeless started to turn up late or miss days of work entirely. It became clear they needed some practical support alongside the job as well as mental health support and we simply didn't have the resources to provide this. These HR issues only led to further financial pressure, weighing heavily on our fledgling social enterprise.

In 2014, we were due to close the shops over the Christmas break, and our cash reserves were close to running dry. I was worried about whether or not we would survive in the new year, genuinely fearful that this whole journey was about to come to a sudden end. We were in need of a Christmas miracle!

Several years before this point, my parents had divorced. It was becoming a bit awkward every Christmas for me and my brother to decide whether to go to my mum's or my dad's house on Christmas Day. This particular Christmas of 2014, I decided to take myself out of that dilemma. So, less out of complete altruism and more to avoid a family drama, you might say, I decided to open up our shops in Edinburgh and Glasgow on Christmas

Paying it Forward

Day and put on a Christmas dinner service for people who were homeless. Given our precarious cash flow situation, I thought I should at least try and cover our costs for running this service, so I reached out to a friend of mine, Oli Norman, who runs a website called itison.com. His website offers daily deals to their customers where you can buy discounted gifts and experiences such as hotel breaks, restaurant offers and many other nice things. I asked Oli if he would consider running a deal where someone could buy someone who was homeless Christmas Dinner for £5. He said, 'Of course I will,' and asked me how many I would like to sell. I suggested that if we could sell 800 dinners for £5 then that would allow us to open up the shops in both Edinburgh and Glasgow. When Oli enquired, 'What happens if we sell more?' I explained the situation with the Pay It Forward jars running empty and suggested we could top them up for a few weeks or months to help us feed people into the new year. Oli agreed and we launched the deal two weeks before Christmas.

We all sat with our fingers crossed as the deal went live on Oli's website. We hoped we'd be able to sell those 800 dinners as planned. We watched on in amazement. The site sold 800 dinners in only ten minutes! *Holy shit*, I thought. *What is happening?* The deal ran for two weeks and ended up selling 36,000 dinners and raised £180,000. Right on cue, our Christmas miracle had arrived!

I suppose that, as they say, fortune does favour the brave. You could argue that while this might seem like a Christmas miracle, in fact it took a whole lot of hard work, lateral thinking, creativity and passion in order for it to appear. Or maybe, it really was just a miracle and we had very little to do with it!

Pray for miracles

In any case, this moment reinforced my belief in the true kindness of people. We opened the door for people to do something kind at Christmas and they kicked that door wide open and surpassed my wildest expectations of what might happen. The kindness and compassion of people when given the opportunity to show it is something that I have seen again and again over the years and it always inspires, amazes and encourages me.

The deal with itison.com is one clear example among hundreds I could share that demonstrates the magic that happens once we commit to our idea. We have run the same partnership with itison. com every year for the last five years and more people have donated every Christmas. The most recent deal sold 101,000 dinners. From that Christmas in 2014 onwards, Social Bite has never had to turn away a single person in need from getting free food in any of our cafes, as the jars are effectively topped up all year round. We now give out over 140,000 items of food and hot drink every year, which are all fully funded.

The funding has also allowed us to invest in a strong support system for our more vulnerable employees, rather than the naive approach we took initially. People coming to work for us from vulnerable backgrounds now get extensive 'wrap-around' support alongside their job. This means that they can receive counselling as well as practical help with opening a bank account, budgeting their money, supporting their housing needs and all other areas they might need assistance with. We have now created 'The Social Bite Academy' for people who were homeless: a short-term six-week training programme, as well as a longer-term, 21-month structured paid employment programme, reinforced with all of the above support to help people sustain their jobs. Over 100 people have now come through the academy and the programme leads the way internationally in delivering a successful employability model for people who are homeless at scale. We have also recently started working with major private sector employers to open up similar employment chances in their businesses (Social Bite provide the support alongside the jobs) which has proved to be a great success.

Pray for miracles

Lesson: Pray for miracles

I have come to believe very strongly in the idea of serendipity or providence. I don't understand how or why it happens, but I believe that if you set out to do something for the common good and you are committed beyond the point of no return, then the universe, God, your lucky stars or whatever higher power you might believe in, will in some way conspire in your favour. In my experience, if you can manage to navigate your life to align with what you believe is your purpose, then all kinds of little miracles will come your way to aid you on your journey. The key is to commit. It is scary, but it is only after you have made the leap of faith and there is no turning back that you can expect something or someone to catch you. There is a quote from a Scottish mountaineer called William H Murray that stuck with me and sums this idea up: 'Until one is committed, there is hesitancy, the chance to draw back, always ineffectiveness. Concerning all acts of initiative and creation, there is one elementary truth, the ignorance of which kills countless ideas and splendid plans: that the moment one definitely commits oneself, then providence moves too. All sorts of things occur to help one that would never otherwise have occurred. A whole stream of events issues from the decision, raising in one's favour all manner of unforeseen incidents, meetings and material assistance which no man could have dreamed would have come his way.

'Whatever you can do or dream you can, begin it. Boldness has genius, power and magic in it. Begin it now.'

Putting it into practice

1. Realise that all entrepreneurs come to so-called crisis points: it's in the very nature of being an entrepreneur and pushing boundaries. The real test is in how you react.

2. Think laterally: sometimes the best solutions can come from left field. Never forget the true kindness of people. If you tilt the door for people to get behind your vision and express their own kindness, they will likely kick that door wide open and surpass your wildest expectations.

3. Use your network to find a spark that might become a miracle. If I hadn't reached out to my friend Oli Norman and his website, itison.com, Social Bite might not have survived to tell the tale, or at the very least we would be a very different organisation today. Creating a strong network of collaborators is absolutely vital to the success of your organisation.

4. As soon as you have committed to your idea beyond the point of no return, then providence will move too, and all sorts of things will occur that you couldn't have dreamed possible. Aim high, and you will achieve high too.

Chapter 8

Find your compassion

Jim's story

I never like to paint too rosy a picture of our work at Social Bite; I feel that it is important to highlight some of the challenges with creating a social enterprise. I tell this story to highlight some of the difficult management challenges we face in running an enterprise like Social Bite and some of the complexities of bringing excluded people into your workforce. The story also serves to illustrate the importance of leading with compassion at the heart of your decision making. This is a story about an employee who had once been homeless. I will call him Jim here in the interests of preserving anonymity.

For several months in 2014, we had an issue with theft. Things kept going missing. One day we cashed up and realised that £20 had been stolen from the till. Several days later, £10 went missing from a member of staff's wallet. Soon after, somebody's iPod went missing. It was apparent that someone was stealing from us and their colleagues. There were a few people we suspected it might be, but this particular employee, Jim, didn't really spring to mind. He was such a warm, friendly man we just did not suspect it could be him. However, as time went by, the coincidences kept stacking up. Whichever shop Jim was working in, whichever shift he was scheduled to work, it corresponded to when things would go missing. After a while, we had reached the conclusion that the thief realistically had to be Jim. Although we didn't have any concrete evidence, there was no other logical explanation.

The persistent theft was causing issues and tension with the other employees as no one could trust each other at work and it was undermining team morale. Because of my lack of firm evidence, one day I decided to try and bluff Jim and force an admission from him in order to get to the bottom of it. So, I went into our Shandwick Place cafe in Edinburgh where Jim was working and asked him if we could have a chat. We went and sat in a booth in the cafe, and I sat directly opposite Jim and attempted to get him to admit to stealing. I said, 'Jim, something I haven't told you, I haven't told anyone, is that we have had covert cameras installed in the back of the shop. We have caught you on film stealing from us and stealing from your colleagues. If you admit it now then there will be no consequences and we can support you with whatever it is that you need help with. But if you deny it now, then there will be some really serious consequences.' Jim, who was sitting squarely in front of me in a booth in the cafe, looked me directly in the eyes and he said, 'Show me the footage.' I stared back at him blankly. He continued, 'If you have the footage, show me it. Because I swear to you on my life, it was not me. You have given me this chance, I would

never betray that. I promise you, it is not me that has been stealing.'
I looked Jim in the eyes for a long time and he did not flinch. I
went back to the office that day and said to the team, 'It is definitely
not Jim. He didn't even flinch when I mentioned the cameras. He
swore on his life. It's not him. It must be somebody else.'

Several weeks went by from this conversation and we were still
none the wiser as to who had been stealing. An important area of
the business that we had been developing was outside catering and
the delivery of sandwich platters to local businesses and corporate
companies.

On this particular day, Jim was asked by the shop manager to
deliver a platter of sandwiches to one of our corporate catering
clients, a local law firm called Lindsays. Jim delivered the sandwiches that day, seemingly without any issues. The following day
I was doing routine phone calls to all of our catering clients to
check that they were happy with their food. I phoned this particular law firm and said, 'Hello, I am phoning from Social Bite.
I just wanted to check that everything went OK with your catering yesterday?' The receptionist responded, 'Yes, the food was all
very good, but one issue is that the other receptionist who was
working yesterday . . . well . . . her mobile phone has gone missing. We think whoever dropped off the sandwiches has stolen
her phone.'

I realised it must have been Jim stealing all along. Angry at having the wool pulled over my eyes, I marched into the shop and
said, 'Jim, let's go for a walk.' We walked out of the shop, down
to Princes Street Gardens in the centre of Edinburgh and sat on a
park bench. I tried to look Jim in the eye, but he sheepishly looked

at the ground. I said to him, exasperated, 'You took that woman's phone! And you lied to me.' Initially Jim tried to deny it, but after a while he broke down in tears, got really upset and admitted that he had been the one stealing. What came out that day, which we had not realised before, is that Jim, who by this stage was in his late thirties, had, from the age of 16, developed a really serious gambling addiction. Everything he had been stealing was going straight into Ladbrokes and being gambled on the roulette machines. The receptionist's phone, within 24 hours, had already been pawned and the money had already been gambled away.

At this point we were faced with a difficult dilemma. What should we do? Certainly, my instinct and most of the advice I was given at the time was obviously to sack him. Not only had he broken my trust, he had also broken the trust of his colleagues and it seemed like an almost impossible situation to repair. However, where it gets slightly more complicated is that if you are trying to bring people who have been severely excluded into the workforce, then sometimes you have to try to put yourselves in their shoes and try to understand their behaviour within the context of the lives that they have had.

When Jim was upset and opening up to me that day on a park bench in Princes Street Gardens, I learned more about his personal story, which he subsequently gave me permission to share. Jim's story, as shocking as it is, is not dissimilar to many people that you might meet who end up homeless on our streets. From when he was born to when he was seven, Jim did not grow up with his parents, but with friends of his parents, who were drug addicts and alcoholics. From this young age, Jim and his two siblings used to be

Find your compassion

locked in a small dark room. They were given a bucket to go to the toilet in and fed porridge oats through the door. That was his early childhood. At the age of seven, there was a house fire, where one of Jim's siblings died. Jim and his other sibling then got taken into the care system. He was bounced around different children's homes and foster homes, and at the age of 16, Jim became homeless.

Hearing Jim's story, I thought to myself that I could not even begin to put myself in his shoes. If that has been your childhood experience and you get none of the love or care or nourishment that most of us take for granted, then you would try to find joy, however fleeting, wherever you could. At the age of 16, Jim went into the bookmakers, gambled some money and won. He got that first buzz of joy and adrenalin – is it surprising that this became an addiction?

Around the time that this situation arose, I had heard a quote from a man named Father Gregory Boyle who runs a similar organisation in the USA called Homeboy Industries where they help gang members in Los Angeles gain employment in their social enterprises. Father Gregory's quote really stuck with me; I try to let it inform me and our senior management team when faced with these kinds of dilemmas: 'Here is what we seek: a compassion that can stand in awe at what the poor have to carry rather than stand in judgment at how they carry it.'

When I thought about Jim and all of these people I was meeting from a homeless background, my only rational response was *awe*. I wasn't confident that if it had been me in their shoes, having lived their lives, that I would still be on my feet, let alone turning up to work every day trying to get my life on a better path.

Paying it Forward

With this in mind, what we decided to do with Jim was sus-
pend him for three months. During this time, we helped him find a
local Gamblers Anonymous group which he relished going to every
week. We also realised at this point that the employment alone
was not enough to truly help many of these individuals. We had
to reinforce the job with wider support. So, we started to employ
a local counsellor and support worker called Barbara Haig, affec-
tionately known as Babs, who is still with us to this day and is truly
a guardian angel to many of our more vulnerable employees. After
his three-month suspension, Jim was repositioned with a job in our
central kitchen where he went on to work extremely well for several
years. In 2016, Jim moved on from Social Bite and went on to get
a job for an upmarket hotel on Princes Street in Edinburgh. But
not before he had the privilege of being one of a team of five people
from homeless backgrounds who all cooked lunch for Hollywood
megastar, George Clooney.

Find your compassion

Lesson: Find your compassion

If you are working with vulnerable members of society, you need to try to put yourselves in their shoes and understand their behaviour in the context of the lives they have had.

Remember the words of Father Gregory Boyle and seek to have a compassion that stands in awe of the burdens that the poor have to carry, rather than in judgement at the way that they carry them.

Putting it into practice

1. Compassion over judgement

Compassion is often overlooked in the business world, but it is and should be a core component of being a social entrepreneur and running a social enterprise. A social entrepreneur should be quick to show understanding and slow to pass judgement on others, especially as no one truly knows the experiences of another.

2. Conversation is a way to healing

Conversations can be difficult, and might not always expose someone's truth at the first go – or even the second – but remember that conversation is a way to healing. Trust the process and engage in that tough conversation without delay.

3. Find solutions that work for all parties

In Jim's case, we found a solution that benefitted him, by suspending him for three months while making sure he had the care he needed to overcome his problems. This also benefitted us as he came back to work happier, healthier and was a true asset to Social Bite, before going on to find employment elsewhere.

Chapter 9
If you don't ask, you don't get

Clooney and DiCaprio come to town

In early 2015, I decided to speculatively write a letter to Hollywood icon George Clooney, inviting him to come to Edinburgh and visit our little cafe. In November of that year, our small charity's world was turned upside down when George did just that and travelled all the way to Scotland to visit our Social Bite cafe on Rose Street. Edinburgh is not very used to celebrities visiting the city, let alone megastars like Clooney, so it felt like the whole city came to a standstill and no one could quite believe their eyes, including me! On the day of the event, hundreds of largely female fans had been camping outside the Social Bite cafe since 6am. Hordes of paparazzi and television crews were starting to assemble outside the shop, awaiting the arrival of one of the world's biggest movie stars.

I had approached George Clooney through a charity that he co-founded called Not on Our Watch, an organisation which promotes human rights in the Sudan. At this time, alongside leading Social Bite, I was still organising my Scottish Business Awards event as a major annual fundraising dinner. So, the original focus of my letter was to invite Mr Clooney to follow in the footsteps of Sir Bob Geldof and President Bill Clinton by being the keynote speaker at the dinner, which, by this stage was attracting up to 2,000 guests. So, through a combination of selling tables and with the support of corporate sponsors and philanthropic backers like Sir Tom Hunter and People's Postcode Lottery, we had the capacity to offer a significant donation to George's charity if he could make the time to visit Scotland and be the keynote speaker. His office responded positively and, as it looked likely that he was going to commit to make the trip, I said to his team, 'Look, we also do this social enterprise in Scotland called Social Bite.' I explained the concept and our work and asked if George would be up for spending ten minutes during his trip to visit the cafe. To my absolute delight they said yes. I knew his visit would transform the profile of our charity and in turn elevate the platform we had to help people.

By the time George arrived at lunchtime on Rose Street, the view outside our cafe was like the scene from *Notting Hill* when William Thacker's (Hugh Grant) flatmate Spike, played by Rhys Ifans, steps out of his flat and there is a sea of paparazzi, flashing cameras, news crews and journalists. It felt as though the whole of Edinburgh ground to a halt as people lined the streets and hung out of nearby windows to catch a glimpse of one of Hollywood's biggest stars visiting our humble sandwich shop. George arrived and made time to say hello to everyone who had been waiting to see him, signing autographs and taking photos. When he entered the

If you don't ask, you don't get

shop, he was so courteous with each member of our team, laughing, joking and taking selfies with our employees. He donated $1,000 in cash to the Pay It Forward jar. He then joined us for a private lunch with some of our main supporters, where our employees were able to help prepare the food, in an amazing culmination of their culinary training. We even raffled off 'the chance to have lunch with George Clooney' for £5, which generated over £40,000 of donations! To this day, George remains one of the most genuinely caring, funny and charismatic people I have ever met – every bit the superstar you hope he would be.

The media profile a celebrity visit like that can bring to a small charitable organisation like ours is remarkable. The next day, I went into the local newsagents and to my amazement Social Bite and George Clooney were on the front page of every single national newspaper in the United Kingdom. We were a main news item on the BBC News at 6. I have cousins that live in South Africa who were phoning me up saying, 'We've just seen you on the South African news with George Clooney!' I can only imagine it must have been a slow news day because the story was only really 'GEORGE CLOONEY EATS SANDWICH!' Overnight, almost everyone in the country had heard of Social Bite, and our social enterprise business model. We went from being unheard of, apart from in terms of the immediate localities of the shops, to being a charity known by the whole nation. It gave us a fantastic platform to develop and grow our work. Overnight, new funding opportunities came our way, politicians started to listen to our voice on the homelessness issue and we were overwhelmed by the groundswell of support from the public. It was a game-changer and really demonstrates how celebrity endorsement can have a significant impact on a charity or social enterprise.

In 2016, I decided to see if lightning could strike twice, and I wrote a similar letter to Leonardo DiCaprio through the Leonardo DiCaprio Foundation, which works to tackle climate change. By this stage, we had opened 'Home', an upmarket restaurant in Edinburgh, based on the same principles as Social Bite. I invited Leonardo DiCaprio to visit the restaurant for lunch. I couldn't quite believe it when lightning did indeed strike twice and Leo also said 'yes'. He arrived in Edinburgh on 17 November 2016, almost exactly 12 months after Clooney had, and was greeted by a similar media storm. No one in Scotland could quite understand how these megastars were flocking to this tiny social enterprise. I was fairly gobsmacked myself! As Leo arrived at the restaurant, a man was leaning out of a first-floor window on the street blasting out the *Titanic* theme song, 'My Heart Will Go On' by Celine Dion. A photo was captured of him arriving, with the number 47 bus from Granton behind him at the bus stop, which went viral online with the caption, 'Breaking: Leonardo DiCaprio arrives on the Granton Bus'. You can't beat the Scottish humour.

Leo was an extremely charming and thoughtful man, who inspired us all in Scotland with his passion to protect the environment. He was dressed immaculately in a sharp suit, sporting his trademark goatee, and took great interest in the social enterprise business model we had created, listening intently to all we had to share with him. When I was talking him through our business model he turned to his manager and said, 'Shawn, do you know where we need one of these? Los Angeles.' Leo explained how terrible the homelessness issue is in his home town of LA, where there are around 50,000 people living in a tent city called Skid Row, and he encouraged us to bring the model there. He spent around two hours in the restaurant at a lunch for all of Social Bite's top supporters, where everyone had the opportunity to ask him a question. I recall one of our supporters, John Watson, asking in his booming Glaswegian accent, 'Leo, from all of the films you've done over the years, which would you say has been your most successful?' To which Leo replied, 'That would be a little-known movie called *Titanic*, I'm not sure if you've heard of it?' We also raffled off the chance to have lunch with Leo for £5, and he was happy to hear it raised more than £40,000 and beat George's total!

Leo was equally gracious with all of our team. One of our former employees with a background of homelessness, Biffy, has loved Leo since she was a small girl and couldn't believe it when she had the chance to prepare his lunch, meet him and get a photo with him. She appeared with Leo on the front page of a national newspaper the following morning with the headline being a quote from her saying, 'I used to feel invisible. Now I got to cook lunch for Leonardo DiCaprio.'

After these two remarkably high-profile visits, Social Bite had an amazing presence in Scotland where almost everyone in the country had heard about our work. We had a platform to aim much higher. I wanted to use our new-found profile to raise our ambition and go far beyond offering just food and jobs.

The more I saw the desire to help from all walks of life, the more I believed that we could create a society where no one should have to be homeless. I decided that we should try and get to the root cause and start to build homes to put a roof over people's heads. The visits from Clooney and DiCaprio gave our social enterprise a wider platform and increased public support, encouraging us all to set our aspirations for Social Bite even higher.

Lesson: If you don't ask, you don't get

The reality of modern life is that we live in a celebrity-obsessed world, but all too often, celebrity endorsement points us in the direction of buying a new watch or aftershave. Celebrity endorsement also has the potential to shine a spotlight not only on the work of your organisation, but also on the wider issue that you care about. The media spotlight that George and Leo's visits shone, not only on Social Bite, but on the issue of homelessness, helped to raise awareness and compassion for the issue throughout Scotland.

The impact of this on our social enterprise was that new funding opportunities came our way, including a £500,000 grant from the National Lottery. As well as the financial impact, politicians started to listen to our voice on the homelessness issue, which led to significant and meaningful policy change. Beyond this, the groundswell of support from the public in Scotland is something that the charity still benefits from to this day.

Putting it into practice

1. If you don't ask, you don't get

My approach to both Clooney and DiCaprio was speculative – I could never have dreamed both would take up my invitation. But you will miss 100 per cent of the shots you never take. If you want to make something happen, put yourself out there and see what happens. You will never know until you try.

2. Focus media attention on your cause

Like it or not, we live in a celebrity-obsessed world. We were able to utilise these visits to shine a spotlight on the issue of homelessness and to expand the awareness of what Social Bite were doing. This undoubtedly helped to propel our organisation forward in a way we could have only dreamed about before. Think about how inviting a high-profile person to support your work might help to shine a light on your cause.

3. Use star power as a springboard

A third lesson is to try to use celebrity star power, and all the attention, interest and engagement it generates, as a platform to realise even more ambitious plans in order to succeed in your purpose and in your mission. Always have a plan in place about how you will leverage this extra attention in order to hit your next objective or target.

Chapter 10

It takes a village

The importance of collaboration

There is an oft-cited quote saying, 'If you want to go fast, go alone; if you want to go far, go together.' As the ambition of our work grew, I began to realise that there was a limit to what I could achieve on my own. I didn't have the experience, skills or the time to make significant change without the support of an amazing team and a range of collaborators and partners. It dawned on me that the primary role of an entrepreneur is to set the vision that others can rally around. The entrepreneur should establish the end destination and inspire others to share in the mission to help get there. It is only through teamwork and collaboration that we can make a meaningful difference in the world.

Following the high-profile visits of George Clooney and Leonardo DiCaprio, I was keen to capitalise on our new-found public profile and develop more ambitious projects to tackle homelessness. We had now been working with people who were homeless for over four years and had developed a deep understanding of the problem. I gathered information by asking questions of the people we were offering food or employment to: 'What happens to you when you become homeless?' 'How does the council help you?' 'What kind of accommodation would you have access to?'

What I found out was eye-opening. I learned that when someone finds themselves becoming homeless in the UK, they will typically go and 'present' to their local council's homelessness office and inform them that they have been made homeless. Provided that the individual is a UK citizen, each local government in the UK has a statutory obligation to provide some kind of temporary shelter. I learned that in the UK there are two primary forms of homeless accommodation that people will be placed into if they are not sleeping on the streets. The first is what is known as a 'shelter'. These can take various forms and will range from a church hall with single mats laid out on the floor side by side for everyone to sleep on, to larger-scale hostels where between 20 and 50 people will be congregated together, typically in dormitory rooms or on bunk beds. These forms of accommodation are often completely unsupported, alcohol and drug addiction tends to be rife and they can be extremely intimidating environments, where bullying and abuse is all too common. Many people told us that they would choose to sleep rough in a cold doorway or back alleyway rather than stay in one of the homelessness hostels in order to avoid conflict or drug use, which I suppose tells you everything you need to know about the standard of many of these accommodations. The average time someone would be made to live in accommodation like this could be up to two years before they qualified for a mainstream social tenancy.

The other primary form of homelessness accommodation is known as 'homelessness bed and breakfasts' (B&Bs). B&B can be a misleading term as it may bring up connotations of picturesque tourist accommodation with delicious home-cooked breakfasts in the morning. But homelessness B&Bs are a long way from that. People living in these B&Bs typically get a single bed and a kettle with no other form of cooking facility. I have heard complaints of 'piss-stained mattresses' or 'beds crawling with bedbugs'. Many families with young children are placed in this type of accommodation as well as single people. The B&B accommodation is particularly infuriating because they are almost all run by private landlords, in what is an immoral profit-making scheme, literally created from human suffering. Edinburgh council alone pays out more than £11 million per year to private landlords for this type of accommodation. Typically, not a penny of this money is invested in support for the individuals in need. One of the main B&B landlords in Edinburgh lives in a mansion and drives a Lamborghini, which says it all. The same thing is happening in many of the major cities throughout the UK. The more I learned, the more outraged I was. I thought there must be a better way.

I began to formulate the idea of building a 'village' for people who were homeless. I envisaged some kind of utopia: beautiful homes, sea views, flower and vegetable gardens, comprehensive support to help people find their feet. Why not? My view was that the people who have endured the worst throughout their lives deserve the best in their hour of need. It was surely no more ridiculous than the status quo.

Paying it Forward

Armed with information regarding how much money the council spends on B&Bs and hostels, and fresh from the positive publicity over the George Clooney and Leonardo DiCaprio visits, I approached Edinburgh council and explained that we wanted to develop an alternative model of homelessness accommodation and told them of my ambition to build a village. I was offered a meeting with some senior officials and councillors. I asked them if they had any vacant derelict council-owned land that they could offer us to build a community where people would live and find support. I explained that the idea was that we could construct high-quality, pre-fabricated wooden houses for people to live in a community and invest heavily in a strong support team to help the residents find their feet. I talked them through a vision where we would have a strong focus on helping people into employment or education. I envisaged that people would live there for the exact same amount of time that they would have otherwise been in a hostel or B&B: between eighteen months and two years before transitioning into a more traditional flat. I told the council that we would call it the 'Social Bite Village'.

The council officers responded positively to the proposition and offered to show me around four or five possible plots of land that were derelict around the city. I visited them all and found one in particular that seemed perfect. Located in the north of the city in an area called Granton, it was in an industrial part of town, but the site was next to woodlands and overlooked the waterfront. It felt serene, secluded, peaceful and even had a sea view! While it was secluded, it was also two minutes from a bus stop, a local supermarket and the local college, so it wasn't isolated. I said to the council,

It takes a village

'This is perfect, we'll take it!' We agreed with the council that they would lease us the land for free. We agreed terms on a lease, with a review point after five years.

With any idea, there is a moment where it stops being just an 'idea' and becomes a tangible project that people can start to believe in. Now that we had our land agreed with the council, we had reached that tipping point. I had started to research small architecture models to try to develop what our houses would look like. There are hundreds of designs out there utilising small architecture, from re-formed shipping containers, to tiny houses, to 'prefabs' that were popular in the years following World War II. Architectural television shows like *Grand Designs* often feature innovative ways of creating beautiful living environments for smaller homes. As I began to research different models I decided it was important to avoid ideas like re-forming shipping containers. This is because, as innovative as you can be and as nice as you can make them look, living in a shipping container is still a bit, well, weird. When you think about it, most of us would not want to live in a shipping container, so why would someone who happens to be homeless want to live in one? It was important to me that our houses felt like beautiful homes.

As I was researching architectural models to design our houses, I had assumed that I would have to search all over the world for best practice to find the right model for us. However, serendipity struck again and I received an email from our support worker Babs with a website link to an architect called Jonathan Avery, who is a world-leading specialist in small architecture and is based a mere 20 minutes from Edinburgh, in a town called Linlithgow.

Paying it Forward

I contacted Jonathan and arranged to go and see him at his home a few days later. Jonathan is a quirky and lovable character. To my amazement, he had built a small wooden prototype 'tiny home' in his garden. He called it a 'nest house'. It was beautifully designed, painted a striking red with an outdoor decking and garden furniture.

Jonathan showed me inside to see a small living room, a kitchenette with a dining table, a wood-burning fire and a double bed located up a mini set of stairs on a mezzanine level. It was beautifully created using clever architectural techniques to make the most of the space and had an innovative insulation system making it nice and cosy. It felt like a Scandinavian-style holiday log cabin. I could imagine myself living there!

Jonathan told me of a growing 'tiny house' movement all over the world. After the economic crash in 2008, people began downsizing to tiny homes where they could live mortgage-free. Many first-time buyers who could not get themselves on to the housing ladder were also opting for a tiny house rather than renting all of their lives. The look and feel of the 'nest house' was perfect for our village. We wanted our houses to have two bedrooms each because we could help twice the number of people for a similar cost of construction. So, I asked Jonathan if I could commission him to design a similar version of his 'nest house' for us with two bedrooms. Jonathan loved the idea that his architecture and design principles could be put to use to help people in need, so he happily agreed and got to work on a new design for us.

Now that we had secured some land and had a vision for the design of the houses, the next challenge was to raise the money to afford the construction of the project. We estimated that it was going to cost around £1.5 million to build 11 houses and a central community hub on the vacant land. With almost nothing available for this project in the charity's bank account, we had a mountain to climb, one that was over and above our day-to-day work. By this time, I had built a large network of CEOs and business leaders in Scotland through our Scottish Business Awards event. I was thinking of a way to engage these affluent and influential people to raise the funds required to construct the village when, suddenly, an idea hit me. I would ask them all to sleep outside for one night on a cold, Scottish winter's evening, to experience a small glimpse into the realities of being homeless and to raise money to help us build the village.

Where did this idea come from? Sometimes ideas will come through a structured brainstorming process, with a team of people round the table and a clear objective. For me though, some of the best ideas often just come to me seemingly from nowhere. Sometimes I will be lying in bed, unable to sleep, and an idea that solves a big problem I have been contemplating for a while just pops into my head. I then won't be able to sleep because I am so excited! I am not 100 per cent sure of the psychology behind this phenomenon, but I guess when you are an entrepreneur, your business or social enterprise will consume a lot of your waking thoughts. Your mind will constantly be whirring away, thinking about your challenges and how to solve them. So, I believe that while this is happening consciously and you don't have the answers, your subconscious mind will be processing in the background all of the time, and then, just when your mind is on something else, it serves you a winning idea for solving a challenge or taking your venture to the next level. I think that this strange phenomenon was at work here.

So, my plan was to ask all the business leaders I had met through my Scottish Business Awards event to sleep outside for one winter's night, to put themselves in the shoes of those who have no choice but to sleep out every night. And given these business leaders were likely to have wealthy friends, I would ask them to raise sponsorship to sleep out. I sent off emails to some of Scotland's top business people and secured Charlotte Square in Edinburgh for the event. That would be the place where the 'CEO Sleepout', as I had decided to call it, would be held. CEOs from major banks, technology companies, property tycoons and start-up entrepreneurs from all over Scotland started to sign up to take part. While this came together very quickly, people's willingness to take part did not surprise me. In fact, I had fully expected it. By this time, I had become used to people from all walks of life – whether a CEO of a FTSE company or a school kid – blowing me away with their kindness and willingness to help. The UK's greatest ever Olympic athlete at the time, Sir Chris Hoy, signed up to sleep out, which really helped us to gather momentum and engage even more business leaders. It was the world's most unusual business networking event!

The CEO Sleepout took place on 15 December 2016, with 270 business leaders sleeping out in the cold. We had some local musicians and comedians come along to keep people entertained until around midnight, when everyone started to bed down for the night. The First Minister Nicola Sturgeon came along in the morning to serve the bacon rolls! To my absolute delight and amazement, those 270 individuals managed to raise £570,000 in one night. We were on our way to building a village and had enough money to get the ball rolling.

Like with most of my working life, I approached this construction project from a position of complete naivety. *It can't be that hard to build a village*, I thought! But of course, I soon came to realise that in fact it was very hard, with many complexities that I had no clue about. One of Social Bite's board members, the late Daniel Muir, had realised that I might be a bit out of my depth. He introduced me to an experienced project manager in the construction industry called Gill Henry for some advice. Gill's day job was as project director of a company called Cruden Homes, one of Scotland's largest house builders. I met with Gill and some of the other directors of Cruden Homes and explained what we were hoping to achieve. Gill and her colleagues quickly realised just how far out of my depth I was, but they saw the vision and wanted to help. Cruden Homes agreed to pay for Gill to be seconded to us as our project director to take the lead on the construction.

Gill quickly ascertained that we didn't have anywhere near enough resources or expertise to successfully build the village. She said that we would need a firm of architects to design the layout for the village and draw up the site plans. I asked her if she knew any architectural companies that might be able to lend a hand and come on board. Gill promised that she would phone a firm she knew called Fouin and Bell, who quickly offered to volunteer their services. We also soon realised that there were contamination issues with the land that the council had offered us and we needed a civil engineer to carry out a significant amount of work to ensure that it would be possible for us to build the village there. Gill contacted an engineering firm called Will Rudd Davidson that she worked with regularly on commercial projects and they quickly agreed to offer their services pro bono, too. I was starting to see the human spirit and compassion snowball again and we had the beginnings of a team assembling to make this project happen.

Given the total cost of the project was costed out at £1.5 million and we had only raised £570,000, it still seemed like we had Everest to climb to make the vision of the village a reality. We had a snowball of support starting to build, but in reality, we needed an avalanche.

We had decided that the houses would follow Jonathan Avery's design principles and would be made out of timber. A few years earlier, I had met a man called Tony Hackney who is at the helm of a large national timber company called BSW Timber. I reached out to Tony and met him for a coffee to explain our plans and to see if he could help. Tony is one of the friendliest people you could hope to meet – a salt-of-the-earth Yorkshireman – and he immediately bought into the vision. He told me on the spot that he would donate all the timber we needed to build the houses. I was blown away; this gesture would substantially reduce the cost of construction. While I was in the process of profusely thanking Tony, he stopped me and said, 'Hang on a minute. Do you need windows?' Confused, I replied, 'Yes, of course.' Tony grinned and said, 'I know some lads that do windows,' in his booming Yorkshire accent. 'Wow,' I said, not quite believing we had potentially secured both timber and windows for free in the same meeting. Maybe we could pull off this ambitious project after all! Tony stopped me again: 'Come to think of it, I also know some lads that do roofs!' he bellowed. 'Do you need roofs?'

It takes a village

And so the snowball grew into an avalanche, as one supplier in the construction industry contacted another one of their peers and more products, materials, expertise and services were donated, completely free of charge. By the time construction was ready to begin, over 30 companies from the construction industry had contributed everything you could imagine, from furniture to paint to a major groundworks operation. I encouraged some generous people I had met along the way to 'sponsor' each of the houses for £30,000 each. We put a small plaque up on each house thanking them for their support, and this added some more funding to the pot.

In the end, the £1.5 million project ended up costing us only around £850,000 because there were so many donated goods and services incorporated into the supply chain. I was blown away by the support. But in a way, I wasn't surprised. I had come to realise that human beings are fundamentally good. All this project did was allow a group of people from a particular industry to come together to use their skills, their products and their expertise to bring something good to fruition. When each supplier chipped in their little bit, it added up to bringing the entire project to life. As they say, it takes a village! In our case it took a village to build a village. We simply nudged the door open for people to express their compassion and, once again, it slammed wide open beyond my wildest expectations.

We commissioned a company in the Highlands of Scotland called Carbon Dynamic, who specialised in pre-fabricated house building, to construct the nest houses. They were constructed in a factory near Inverness and, once completed, the houses were each loaded on to a low-loader lorry and driven across Scotland to the village site. They were then craned into position and connected to electricity, water, drainage and sewage facilities that had been put in place by the groundworks team. The sight of 11 nest houses travelling on low-loader lorries back to back across Scotland, over the Forth Road Bridge towards Edinburgh, is something I will never forget.

As the village development was under way, a strange thing started to happen that I had not anticipated. A homelessness academic and certain other homelessness charities started to publicly criticise the project, all without asking for any specific details about what we had planned. An academic from Heriot-Watt University, who specialises in homelessness, wrote a very strongly worded blog about the project, saying that the village would turn out to be a 'ghetto' and that although we were 'well-meaning' and had 'celebrity support', it would not work and would be detrimental to people who were homeless. In the blog, the academic proactively encouraged people not to support us. Because of our recent high-profile visitors, the media jumped on this, with various papers running a story that 'Leonardo DiCaprio-backed project SLAMMED by homelessness expert'.

Things got stranger still when some other homelessness charities jumped on the bandwagon and started to openly criticise us in the media. I found this all very peculiar because we had not released any public information about the specifics of the programme so, from my perspective, the critique was based on pure conjecture. The critics didn't seek any information about the architecture, the location, the support model or the resources we would invest. The focus of the criticism was that the village would be an environment that grouped people who were homeless together and the fear again was that this would create a 'ghetto' environment. Instead of this model, it was argued that we should be investing funds in a different model that placed people who were homeless directly into mainstream tenancies with support, a model known as 'Housing First'. The ironic thing is that we were also passionate advocates of the Housing First model (it is the subject of Chapters 12 and 13 of this book); we just didn't see it as mutually exclusive with what we were seeking to create with the village. I saw both models as complementary solutions. We knew that if we managed to execute the village project well, we would not create a *ghetto* but instead create a *community*. A place where people could receive support, build positive relationships and find their feet before moving on. Rather than engage in a war of words, we took a deep breath and decided to press on. I was confident in what we were planning and I thought that the only way to respond to criticism would be to make the project successful. The testimony of the residents who lived there would be all that mattered. I was confident we could create a beacon of light in tackling homelessness and provide an alternative to the dreadful status quo homelessness accommodation – and I was more determined than ever to do so.

Just prior to the launch day of the village, we had our whole team on site, applying the finishing touches. Traditional homelessness accommodation is often very run-down. This sends a very subtle but crystal-clear message to those who live there: 'You are not of value; you will get the bare minimum because that is all you deserve.' We wanted to turn that psychology on its head, so we got to work. We planted thousands of beautiful plants and flowers in the flower patches outside the houses. I drove back and forth to

B&Q and Homebase to load up a van with hundreds of plants until I felt we had enough. We went to a large discounted furniture and homeware shop called The Range and loaded up vans with decorations. We invested heavily in little things that were non-essential; nice-to-haves, but not totally required. That was the point. Little signs with inspirational quotes to hang up. Decoration letters that spelled out the word 'HOME' on them. Quirky ornaments, paintings, pictures, mirrors and clocks to hang on the walls.

Inside the homes too, we wanted to make them as functional as possible. I wanted to install wood-burning stoves in each of the houses but I was vetoed on health and safety grounds. So, I insisted that we get fire simulation heaters shipped over from Italy because they had a 'hyper-realistic' flame effect and I wanted people living there to have the sense of a real wood-burning fire. The subconscious message we wanted people to receive was that they were valued and that we trusted them with valuable things. Alongside the nest houses, a large central 'community hub' was constructed, fitted with a large kitchen, dining tables to fit at least 30 people at one time, a large living room area with a real wood-burning fire and an office for support staff. This hub had a large outdoor decking area with a beautiful sea view. The place didn't feel like homeless accommodation at all and it felt a million miles away from the 'ghetto' that some critics had predicted; it felt more like a Scandinavian holiday village.

We launched the village in May 2018 on a gloriously sunny day. I was so unbelievably proud of the project and grateful for the support that rallied round to make it what it became. It had turned out a hundred times better than even I had envisaged. It felt serene and rehabilitative. The houses looked stunning, their unique architecture highlighted by the beaming sunshine, surrounded by freshly planted flowers.

Hundreds of people came to the launch to see what had been created. Attendees included government ministers, supporters of the project, the CEOs that slept out to raise funds, council officials, well-wishers and sceptical citizens from the local community. The media came in their multitudes to see the project and explore the houses and community hub. It was the first project of its kind globally. We allowed people to view the houses, wander round and spend time in the community hub. We had a series of speeches from local people who were homeless, and from me and other members of the team and partners, to thank people for getting involved. Everyone in attendance that day was blown away. People who had arrived feeling sceptical left feeling uplifted, and the media reported on what a fantastic project had been created. I was filled with relief, delight and gratitude that we had made it to this stage. But the hard work was only just beginning as the first residents were due to move in a few weeks later and it would stand or fall on their experience of the village.

We commissioned a local charity called the Cyrenians who have 50 years' experience in community-based support models, led by a wonderful charity leader called Ewan Aitken, to be on site to deliver the support. They recruited five full-time, experienced support staff to deliver one-to-one support as well as to organise fun activities, links to employment and to foster a sense of community. I am very grateful to the Cyrenians for their collaboration on the project as they have done a remarkable job in supporting people as they gradually began to move in.

Paying it Forward

The project has now been running for almost five years and I am thrilled to say that it has been a remarkable success. Almost 100 people have now been helped out of homelessness through the project. I was humbled to hear some of them describe the village as their sanctuary, as they found their feet and broke their individual cycle of homelessness. Many residents are now in employment or have enrolled in the local college and I love going to visit the village to see how everyone is getting on and see them make the place their own.

I believe that the project is by far the most effective form of temporary homeless accommodation in Edinburgh, although that is not difficult given the standard of competition. Following the success of the project, new villages are now in development in Greater Glasgow and Dundee, and we expect to break ground this year in 2023, with the Dundee project being created as a residential recovery facility for people who are homeless and who struggle with addiction issues.

It takes a village

Lesson: No man is an island

The key lesson from this experience is that it is impossible to achieve anything meaningful on your own: you need collaborators. On our own, we were naive, clueless sandwich shop owners with no experience in realising a construction project. But we managed to get everyone, from architects to engineers to timber merchants to window companies, to rally round the project to help bring it to life. In the end, over 50 companies had either donated time, expertise, products or funding towards the project. It all started with Gill Henry, the project director agreeing to get involved and the support snowballed from there. Without that collaborative effort, it simply would not have happened. My role was to galvanise the willing parties around a tangible vision. In the end, it took a village to build the village.

Putting it into practice

1. Collaboration – it takes a village

So, when you are embarking on an ambitious project of your own, you may feel out of your depth, but work on inspiring collaborators to join you. Recruit one or two like-minded people with the skills you need and start rolling your snowball down the hill. Before you know it, the snowball will grow in size and you might just create an avalanche! In the end, you will have an amazing number of collaborating partners, all working together to bring your vision to life. In my experience, people are inherently good. If you give people a project they can apply their skills to with a clear end result of making the world a better place, you will never be short of willing supporters and your project will be much better than it ever could have been without them.

2. Build a team

The same principle goes for employing a team of people around you. One of the special things about founding a charity or social enterprise is that there are thousands of people out there who are passionate about changing the world too. When you first start out, it can sometimes feel like all of the responsibility to make things happen sits with the founding entrepreneur. As time has gone on, I have realised that my main role is to build a team and empower them to deliver the vision. As a charity or social enterprise, you can find incredibly talented and motivated people to come and work with you to bring your vision to life. Social Bite have a truly incredible team of dedicated and talented people, without whom we simply couldn't achieve any of our objectives. So get focused on building your team and you will go far together.

3. Think big

Just because something hasn't been done before, it doesn't mean it can't be done. In the case of the village, there were logistical and financial challenges to make it work, but also it was evident that no organisation had yet tried to provide housing of this quality for rough sleepers and people who are homeless in a community environment with on-site support. We thought big and proved that we could make it happen. If you believe in your vision, don't let critics knock your confidence. The only critics that ultimately matter are the people that you are helping.

Chapter 11

There is no 'them' and 'us'.
There is only 'us'

Sleep in the park

Over the years, I have come to the conclusion that, although in this age of social media we are often divided into increasingly entrenched tribes – Conservatives or Labour; Republicans or Democrats; have or have-nots; 'woke' or 'anti-woke' – in reality there is actually no meaningful separation between us as human beings. There is a lot more that unites us than divides us: there is no 'them' and 'us', but only 'us'.

This viewpoint has been borne out almost every day of my life as I have pursued my work in social entrepreneurship, and I continue to witness the goodness of people each day and a desire to help those suffering in all walks of life. Experiences like the itison.com Christmas campaign or the collaborative support we received to create the Social Bite Village had made my faith in human connectivity unshakeable. The more human kindness I encountered, the more I believed that there was no reason why we could not collectively create a society where no one should have to be homeless at all. I decided to try and bring the whole country together and create a collaborative movement, calling for an end to homelessness in Scotland once and for all. I didn't know it at the time, but this movement would grow all over the world, becoming the largest ever global campaign aiming to end homelessness.

Relatively speaking, Scotland is a small country. We have a population of 5.4 million people, which means that our whole country is smaller than London. Living in Scotland, you are only ever a couple of connections away from the First Minister, or city council leaders, or the leaders in the business community. It really is a village.

Over the course of a year, there are around 35,000 people who become homeless in Scotland. If you take a snapshot on an average night, there will be around 11,000 people who are homeless here, primarily living in temporary accommodation like the B&Bs or shelters. Over the course of a year, around 5,300 people will typically sleep on the streets in the country.

When I began to think about those homelessness statistics within the context of the incredible generosity and support that I had encountered, it dawned on me that these numbers were not that big. In fact, they suddenly seemed like very small numbers indeed. With everything that I had experienced over the years, I fundamentally believed that we could create a collaborative movement in Scotland to drive these numbers right down and create a society where no one should be homeless at all. It seemed to me that with the right tools, it could be possible to eradicate homelessness from the country altogether.

Carefully, I considered how to build this sense of a movement. I decided to try to create an event that would bring many thousands of people from all walks of life together to call for an end to homelessness. Furthermore, the event should raise some significant funding to create projects that would make a dent in our homelessness numbers.

With these objectives in mind, I remembered the success of our 'CEO Sleepout' event, which raised funds to build the Social Bite Village project; I thought this would be a good event concept to build on to create a mass participation campaign. Many questions raced through my mind. Would it be possible to persuade thousands of people from all walks of life to sleep out en masse? Could we raise the funds needed to make a big difference? Would it create the empathy and awareness required to put homelessness at the top of the political agenda? I felt that we could achieve something really special by creating a mass participation sleep out so I decided to put on a major event called 'Sleep in the Park'.

I reached out to Edinburgh council to secure a venue for the event and managed to agree terms to take on the city's main park, Princes Street Gardens. This is the park where Edinburgh's annual New Year's Eve Hogmanay concert and fireworks display happens with a capacity of 10,000 people. We managed to book out Princes Street Gardens for Saturday, 9 December 2017, which was likely to be a very cold Scottish winter's night.

In order to get the public engaged in the event, I decided we would try to put on a major concert before people slept out and

Paying it Forward

I also wanted to find a high-profile person to come and tell the crowd a 'bedtime story' before they bedded down for the night. A year or so prior, I had been invited for dinner with Ricky Ross and Lorraine McIntosh, the lead singers of Deacon Blue, an extremely popular Scottish rock band who rose to prominence in the eighties but who have enduring popularity. I reached out to Ricky to ask if I could meet him for a coffee and we met a few days later in a cafe in Glasgow. Ricky is a truly lovely man and when I told him what we had planned, he immediately pledged his support. He called the rest of the band and confirmed that they would perform, which gave us our first big-name music act. As with most things in life, the hardest part is often getting the first name confirmed, but with Deacon Blue on board, we started to reach out to others and managed to secure a star-studded line-up of performers that included Amy Macdonald and Frightened Rabbit. We even managed to secure one of my favourite rock stars of all time, Liam Gallagher, to agree to come and headline the concert. To top it all off, the comedy legend John Cleese agreed to come and be the 'bedtime storyteller' before partici-pants slept out for the night.

With this amazing array of musicians performing and a bedtime story from John Cleese confirmed, in early September 2017 we were ready to announce the event to the public. This gave us only three months to persuade thousands of people to sleep out with us on a cold winter's night to raise the funds and awareness nec-essary to make inroads into tackling homelessness. Our target was to have 8,000 people come and sleep out en masse and we decided to set a massively ambitious fundraising target of £4 million for the campaign. I had no idea if we could achieve this, but I had developed a strong conviction that the vision could be manifested into reality and that once we committed, little miracles would occur in our favour to help make it happen.

In order to participate in the event, people had to commit to raising a minimum of £100. I had spoken with a concert promoter friend of mine who told me that, when promoting concerts for a big music artist, they would typically sell 50 per cent of their tickets on launch day in order to get a sell-out event. On that basis, on the day we launched the campaign we were really hoping to secure 4,000 registrations (50 per cent of the 8,000-participant target) to give us a good chance of selling the event out.

We had a press launch where we promised the media details of a major new event. I was relieved to see that all of the local newspaper journalists, photographers and TV crews arrived, all intrigued by what we were going to announce. The launch of the campaign was widely covered in all of the media and I eagerly ran back to the office at the end of the day to check how many people had signed up to sleep out, keeping my fingers crossed that several thousand people would have registered. My heart sank when my colleagues told me the numbers – only 100 people had signed up on the first day. I was terrified. We had booked out the largest park in the city, had a star-studded line-up and had invested significant funds to create this major event – it would be an absolute disaster if barely anyone decided to sign up to participate. It seemed like we had another mountain to climb. I had committed to this: I had jumped off the cliff and passed the point of no return. I really needed people to catch me.

Paying it Forward

I began to reach out to people I had met over the years to tell them what we had planned and asked for their support. I told people that I believed that we could bring an end to homelessness in Scotland, but we needed people to come together to take a stand. I phoned business leaders and asked if they could sign up teams of employees from their workplaces. People started to register teams of five or ten people. I then began to approach the churches, the mosques and the temples to ask if congregations could get involved and sleep out in solidarity with those who had no other choice. As the snowball started to grow, I reached out to the university deans and asked them to get their students involved. Next were the high schools to invite senior pupils. We then went to the government and asked for civil servants and ministers to join; we even said we wanted First Minister Nicola Sturgeon and all the cabinet ministers to sleep out. The snowball grew into another avalanche as more and more people from all walks of life signed up to take part. Our faith was being rewarded.

By the time 'Sleep in the Park' arrived on Saturday, 9 December 2017, 8,000 people had agreed to sleep out. As we got closer to the event, we began to receive weather warnings from the Met Office and local police. As fate would have it, that particular night turned out to be the *coldest* night of the whole year. Temperatures dropped to −8 degrees Celsius. *Would people still show up to take part in these freezing cold conditions?* I wondered. To my amazement every single one of the 8,000 people that had signed up dutifully arrived on the night to sleep out under the stars. After stirring performances from Deacon Blue, Amy Macdonald and Liam Gallagher and a truly bonkers bedtime story from John Cleese, everyone made their way to bed down, side by side. It was incredible to see the sea of people wrapped up in winter gear lying next to each other – schoolchildren and pensioners, business tycoons, bankers and charity workers, government ministers, university students and people from homeless backgrounds, Christians, Muslims and Sikhs – all sleeping out in unison. It was a sight to behold.

We are often told in this life that there is 'us' and 'them'. It can sometimes be easy to categorise ourselves into tribal groups and we can often see people from a different socio-economic background, political affiliation, race or religion as the 'other'. This sense of tribalism is exacerbated by social media and the echo chambers that it creates, where we only speak to people who agree with our point of view. However, when I saw those 8,000 people from every walk of life you could imagine, lying side by side, shivering together in the sub-zero conditions, all to take a stand for the most vulnerable among us, I knew for sure that there is no such thing as 'them' and 'us'. There is only 'us'.

Each of the 8,000 participants had been given an online fundraising page prior to the event and we encouraged them all to fundraise as much as they could. For most of the time during the campaign our fundraising target of £4 million seemed incredibly unrealistic. But in the final few days, each participant worked remarkably hard on their fundraising and as people saw the temperatures drop, the donations flooded in. The majority of funds were raised in the final week running up to the event. I was sent the final fundraising total just before I stepped on the stage on the night of the event and the total was £3.97 million. I was blown away. We had hit our target and I knew that this money would make a major difference to the lives of thousands of people who were homeless throughout the country. However, quite apart from the money raised, the 8,000 people who gave up their beds on that cold night created a tangible sense of political urgency. Such a mass display of solidarity, in such cold conditions, is very different from thousands of people signing a petition on an issue. Fully 8,000 people sleeping out in sub-zero temperatures created a clear mandate in Scotland for political action regarding homelessness.

There is no 'them' and 'us'. There is only 'us'

Lesson: Walk a mile in their shoes

One of the key lessons that this experience taught me was the importance of walking in the shoes of the people you are aiming to help.

At some point during the night, I grabbed my sleeping bag and found a spot in the middle of thousands of others to sleep out. I shivered throughout the night along with everyone else, waking up every ten minutes either because of the cold or because of the bustling noise of the city centre on a busy Saturday night. I rose along with 8,000 others at around 6am with my sleeping bag covered in frost and we all left the park together, shuddering with the cold, to make our way back to our own homes.

Obviously taking part in an event like this is nothing like the actual reality of being homeless. People who are actually homeless haven't just seen a performance from Liam Gallagher or had a bedtime story from John Cleese. People who are actually facing the reality of sleeping rough in cities throughout the UK are not in a managed, secure event space with paramedics and stewards checking in on them. The reality for these people is sleeping in a doorway or back alleyway, where they not only have to contend with the cold, but with the fear of being assaulted, abused or robbed. As I got home to my own flat that morning, jumped in a hot shower and changed into a fresh pair of warm clothes, it really hit me. I could cope with getting through that experience for one night. But when I was home, showered and warm, I could not imagine having to sleep out again for a second night, or a third, without anywhere to warm up during the day or to get a warm shower. On average in the UK, people can be homeless for up to two years! If I had no other option but to sleep out night after night, how long would it take me to go and buy a bottle of cider to escape? Or turn to drugs? How long would it take until I had lost all my confidence? Until I had been completely cut adrift from society as most of us know it? The answer, of course, is not long at all.

I believe that the other 8,000 people who shared that experience with me that night had their eyes opened and their perspectives changed forever in the same way. I still meet people who tell me that they slept out that night and how it fundamentally changed their perspective. Those 8,000 people, from all walks of life, have become passionate advocates for tackling this issue in Scotland and beyond. This was only the beginning of the challenge. The next step was to invest the funds we had raised to try and bring Scotland's homelessness numbers significantly down with immediate effect.

Putting it into practice

1. Understand the scale of your issue

A key lesson from this experience is that once we understood the extent of homelessness statistics in our country, we were able to unite people behind the idea that we could end homelessness in Scotland. Scotland is a proud and innovative nation, so we galvanised people when we asked the question, 'Why can't Scotland end homelessness?' So, understand the scale of the issue you are trying to tackle and inspire people with the idea that they can collaborate to solve the problem entirely.

2. Start a movement from all walks of life

One of the most amazing things about Sleep in the Park was in witnessing 8,000 people from different walks of life sleeping side by side in solidarity with the most vulnerable people in society. Think about how you can bring people from different cross-sections of society together to unite behind your cause. By doing so you can get the attention of your political leaders and demand action on your issue.

3. Walk in the shoes of the people you are helping

The experience of sleeping out allowed us, for one night, to experience a small glimpse into the hellish realities of what people who are homeless go through every night. This taught me the importance of walking in the shoes of the people you are aiming to help. The realisation of this will help drive you forward in your mission.

Chapter 12
Find global solutions

How to end homelessness

Sometimes the social problems we face can feel intractable. When you are embarking on your own journey to make a difference, the scale of the challenge might feel impossible. People often ask me if I really believe it is possible to end homelessness. Just walking the streets of major cities in the UK can make the situation feel hopeless: we all see countless people on our way to work who are sleeping rough or begging on the pavements. The problem has become visibly worse over the past few years, having been compounded by years of austerity policies. Alongside the economics of austerity implemented by the Conservative government from 2010, factors including upward pressure on housing costs, reduced availability of affordable social housing since the early 1980s, reduced funding for supporting vulnerable people with their housing – cut by 59 per cent in real terms since 2010 – and restrictions on housing benefit for lower income families, have led to an explosion of homelessness in the UK.

The statistics back this up, not only in the UK, but all over the world. In the last two years alone the number of people sleeping rough in the UK rose by 7 per cent. In Germany, the last two years saw a 35 per cent increase in the number of people who are homeless, while in France, there has been an increase of 50 per cent in the last 11 years. In one of the most iconic and affluent cities in the world, New York, there are more people experiencing homelessness than at any time since the Great Depression. In a city of more than 8.4 million people, nearly 1 in every 125 New Yorkers is homeless: that's nearly 70,000 men, women and children. California has seen the largest spike to its homeless population ever, with an increase of 21,306 people in 2019, making the Golden State's total homeless population roughly 151,278 people in 2019.

These are some of the world's biggest economies with immense wealth, and yet they haven't solved their housing problem. Indeed, the problem is getting worse. Across the world, the picture is much the same. In the face of these statistics it may seem unrealistic or even naive to imagine that we could end homelessness in our society. But I believe that there is hope. I believe this because there is one country that has managed to reverse this global trend and seen homelessness statistics significantly drop each year over the last decade. That country is Finland.

So, what have Finland been doing differently?

It turns out that it has pretty much done the opposite of what everywhere else in the world has done and turned the traditional approach to tackling homelessness on its head. The way we have

Find global solutions

Graph 3. Long-term homelessness in PAAVO municipalities 2008-2016

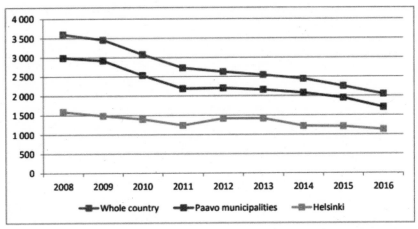

traditionally tackled homelessness in the UK – and in most of the world's major economies – is by giving a person a home as the final point of intervention. There are many reasons why someone becomes homeless, including childhood trauma, job loss, family breakdown, addiction to drugs or alcohol or mental health problems. Most homelessness policies work on the proviso that the individual must be 'tenancy ready': the notion that the person has to solve these challenges in their life first before they can get permanent accommodation. Put simply, people who are homeless have to prove that they have tackled and solved their mental health, addiction or employment issues before they qualify to be trusted with their own permanent tenancy.

But common sense will tell you that this policy is back to front. If you are homeless, then your mental health is likely to deteriorate pretty rapidly and keep getting worse. You are more likely to develop addiction issues and these are likely to compound. As each day passes, you risk becoming further removed from mainstream society, as your self-confidence diminishes and you become increasingly stigmatised.

My experience of sleeping out for one night for 'Sleep in the Park' showed me how much your mental health could be affected by sleeping out on a cold winter's night, and that had been for just one night. In the UK, someone who is homeless is likely to remain so for an average of up to two years. So, the concept of asking people to prove themselves to be 'tenancy ready' while making them live in a situation that sends them on a downward spiral is fundamentally flawed.

Finland does the opposite: it gives people who are homeless a home *first*. The scheme, introduced in 2007, is called Housing First. It is built on the principle that a person can only manage to solve the challenges they face in their lives once they have a stable base to call home. Only by having a permanent home can they even begin to solve mental health or addiction challenges, or start to think about finding a job. With this fundamental base of a home for people, the government then invests in a 'wrap-around' support to help the individual overcome any of the challenges they may face in their lives. This support is tailored to each person's specific situation. It could be mental health support and counselling, or addiction therapy or practical things like helping them open a bank account or making sure they have food in the fridge and some company every day. How do you end homelessness? Simple really: just give people a home and a bit of support. It really is not rocket science.

In Finland, when someone becomes homeless, they are not made to live on the streets, or in the unsupported hostels or exploitative

Find global solutions

B&Bs for up to two years. Instead, they are given permanent housing on a normal lease. There are no labels. No stigma. They are not cut adrift from mainstream society in the same way people who become homeless are here. Tenants pay rent and are entitled to receive housing benefits. Depending on their income, they may contribute to the cost of the support services they receive. The rest is covered by local government. Since the scheme started in Finland, thousands have benefitted and homelessness statistics have plummeted.

In order to properly execute a Housing First strategy to tackle homelessness, governments must also deal with chronic housing shortages. In Finland, increasing the supply of affordable rental housing was a critical part of the approach. Finland used its existing social housing stock, but also bought flats from the private market and built new housing blocks in order to provide homes. There are no more homeless shelters in Finland: they have all been turned into supported housing.

While this may seem expensive, implementing Housing First actually saves society money compared to the costs of having a significant homeless population. Juha Kaakinen, chief executive of Y-Foundation, a social enterprise that helped to pioneer this model, said,

'All this costs money, but there is ample evidence from many countries that shows it is always more cost-effective to aim to end homelessness instead of simply trying to manage it. Investment in ending homelessness always pays back, to say nothing of the human and ethical reasons.'

After our Sleep in the Park event, where we had managed to raise an incredible amount of money, there was a significant burden of responsibility to invest the funds in the best way. I wanted to make sure that we invested the money in a way that would help the most people out of homelessness, but more than this, I also wanted to use the money to exert influence in changing our government's policy on the issue.

Given that the premise of the Sleep in the Park event was that we could end homelessness in Scotland, we wanted to look at best practice all over the world in how this issue was being tackled and ultimately solved. When we learned about Finland's successful Housing First policy, it was a beacon of light in a world where the issue was largely getting worse. Over a ten-year period, Finland had effectively ended homelessness in their country. Finland has a population of almost 5.5 million people, almost exactly the same as Scotland. If they could end homelessness in their country then I thought that there was absolutely no reason why Scotland could not do the same thing. The path was therefore a clear one: we had to use the funds that we had raised to create a nationwide Housing First programme in Scotland and we had to make sure that this became mainstream government policy.

In order to create a Housing First programme, the main thing you need is obvious: houses. I researched who the biggest landlords in Scotland were and I decided to reach out to Scotland's largest Housing Association, an organisation called Wheatley Group to see if they could help. Wheatley Group own over 40,000 flats and houses in central Scotland, primarily in Glasgow, and they rent these properties out to people from all walks of life. My objective was to see if they could help us create a Housing First model by ring-fencing a stock of their houses for people sleeping rough. I managed to arrange a meeting with Wheatley Group's chief executive, a fantastic leader called Martin Armstrong. Over a coffee, I explained the Housing First model to Martin and how we wanted to pioneer this in Scotland, but that the first thing we needed was houses. I told Martin that if he could provide the houses, we could help to cover the costs for the 'wrap-around support' that people would need to sustain their tenancies, using some of the funds raised through our Sleep in the Park event. To his eternal credit, Martin pledged his support on the spot and sealed the deal with a handshake. He took the idea to his board and phoned me a couple of weeks later to tell me how many properties they could offer us to give rough sleepers a permanent home – 200 houses in Glasgow. *Wow*, I thought, we were up and running and following in Finland's footsteps, and creating out very own Housing First model.

In Scotland, there is a quite an intense rivalry between Glasgow and Edinburgh. Glaswegians seem to resent that Edinburgh is the capital city and those from Edinburgh can have a tendency to look down their posh noses at Glasgow. So, when I approached the leaders of Edinburgh council to tell them about our plans to create a nationwide Housing First programme and that Glasgow had already pledged 200 properties, their interest was immediately piqued. The leaders of the council invited me to present the idea to a coalition of housing providers made up from all the main landlords in the city. I accepted this invitation and went along to a grand room in the City Chambers on the Royal Mile to present the idea to a room made up of the leaders of around 12 major landlords in Edinburgh. I looked out at a room of stony-faced individuals: this model was very counter-intuitive to them and completely contra-dicted the status quo of how they offered houses. They started to ask me questions. Would people be able to sustain their tenancy and pay their rent on time? Would there be problems for the neigh-bours? Would other people think they are 'jumping the queue' to get a house? Do they deserve their own house or are they better suited to living in homeless accommodation? I patiently answered all of their questions, providing detailed evidence of the success of the policy in Finland. I then told them the vital bit of information that would unlock the houses: Glasgow had offered 200 properties! Not to be outdone, the housing leaders conferred and came back to me with an offer of 275 houses. I was delighted: we now had 475 properties pledged for Scotland's most vulnerable people.

Armed with these pledges in Edinburgh and Glasgow, along with a war chest to help pay for the support costs, I approached all of Scotland's other main cities to see if they would like to join the programme. Not wanting to be left out, we soon had another 355 houses pledged in Dundee, Aberdeen and Stirling, bringing the total number of properties available for Scotland's rough sleepers to 830.

This by far exceeded my expectations of what we could have realistically secured for Scotland's rough sleepers. We decided that we would commission local charities in each city and create a coa-lition that would provide support services for the individuals to help them in their new homes. Based on the best practice from Finland, each support worker should have a relatively low number of peo-ple that they are responsible for helping, so that they can provide fairly intense support if it is required. Each support worker should provide help for a maximum of seven vulnerable people so that they can give each person the time that would be needed. Based on this best practice, we created a budget of £6,000 per year for each housed person, to fund the support costs. The flat that people were moving into would be provided by the landlords unfurnished, so we wanted to also provide funding to give people the furniture that we all need in life, so we added £1,500 per person to the budget for furniture, which helped to provide beds, living room furniture, a television, kitchen equipment and some decoration. This gave a total budget for each person housed of roughly £7,500 per year.

When we added up the costs for the support services and the furniture for a three-year period it came out at £9.5 million. We had budgeted between £2-3 million from the funds we raised at Sleep in the Park to fund these costs, which obviously fell significantly short of what would be required to house and support all 830 people. In order to make this programme a reality and house all 830 people, we would have to secure support from the government.

I approached the Housing Minister, Kevin Stewart MSP, and the civil servants responsible for homelessness to explain the programme that we were trying to create and to ask the government to contribute the £6.5 million required to fully fund the programme. They were all aware of the success of Finland in reducing their homelessness numbers and were very supportive of the Housing First model in principle. However, they all seemed to be fairly paralysed by the bureaucracy that underpinned releasing public funds, at least, that's how it seemed to me in my naivety of how the political process worked. I was confused. We were bringing 830 homes and between £2–3 million of privately raised funds to the table; we had a network of charities poised and ready to start delivering the support; and there were around 5,000 people sleeping rough in Scotland per year that desperately needed these houses. What was the hold-up? The government could reduce their rough sleeping numbers by almost a fifth through this one programme alone and could start to restructure the system towards a solution that works. But it felt like this argument was falling on deaf ears with the civil servants and the minister: it felt like all I was encountering was bureaucracy, inaction and reasons why it couldn't be done. I felt like I was banging my head against a brick wall. Each day as I walked to work and passed countless people waking up in door-ways and shivering through the freezing Scottish winter, my frustration grew. I know that there of course has to be due process and diligence when it comes to releasing public funding, but we had 830 empty houses waiting for these people. I just needed the government to grasp the urgency that I am sure they would feel if it was them sitting out in the cold all winter.

I decided to go directly to First Minister Nicola Sturgeon's office and I arranged a meeting with a special adviser that she had called Jeanette Campbell. Jeanette's focus was on homelessness and poverty in Scotland so I went to meet her in the Scottish parliament. I explained to Jeanette that we had 830 properties available and were prepared to commit £3 million of private money to fund the support costs. I conveyed my frustration at the lack of urgency from the government to co-invest in the programme. Jeanette got it straight away. She asked me to talk her through the economic model and to demonstrate how much government funding would be required to house and support all 830 people. I took out my laptop and showed her our costings based on 830 people gradually moving into their new homes and receiving support for the next three years: the total funding required from the Scottish Government would be £6.5 million, alongside Social Bite's £3 million. Jeanette took my proposal straight to the First Minister. From there things moved quickly and I got an email a few weeks later from Jeanette telling me that the government were going to back the programme and advising me to watch the First Minister's speech in parliament later that day. I turned on the news on my television that night to see Nicola Sturgeon give an address to parliament announcing their support of this new Housing First programme. I was eagerly awaiting confirmation of how much they would co-invest in the programme and was delighted when she announced that it would be £6.5 million to the penny. The programme was now fully funded. In spite of my initial frustration at their seeming lack of urgency, I must give absolute credit to the Scottish Government who ultimately dynamically embraced the opportunity we presented and followed through with widespread policy commitments that I believe are already making major inroads into solving the homelessness issue in Scotland, particularly for rough sleepers.

Over the course of the following 12 months, under the leadership of an amazing programme team led by Maggie-Ann Brünjes from Homeless Network Scotland, rough sleepers in Scotland began to move off the streets into their own permanent homes, with a wrap-around support programme to help them sustain it. So far over 600 people have been housed through our pilot programme and over 1,000 people housed through local authorities in Scotland adopting the model too. The tenancy sustainment rate of the programme is over 80 per cent, with the vast majority of people managing to stay in their properties, thanks to the wrap-around support they receive. These high tenancy sustainment rates are consistent wherever Housing First has been tried in the world.

Scotland's Housing First programme is now the largest of its kind in Europe, alongside Finland. The Scottish Government and all 32 local councils have committed to implementing Housing First as the default policy, effectively turning our homelessness system on its head. Over a ten-year period, Scotland plans to abolish and decommission all forms of traditional homelessness accommodation that we know fail people. The government instead aims to help anyone that becomes homeless into their own home and give them the support they need.

So, is it possible to end homelessness? For the 1,000 people who have been housed and supported so far, their homelessness has ended. I believe that as a country we are now on a path to follow in Finland's footsteps and end homelessness in our society. If Scotland can do it, so can any country in the world. Human beings have achieved far more difficult things in our history. Think about the incredible advancements we have made in our world: the technological innovation, the wealth creation, the medical advances, space exploration. In comparison, ending a social challenge like homelessness really is not that difficult. It is simply a matter of doing things differently, turning the status quo on its head and enacting policy that we know works. It turns out the way to stop people being homeless is pretty simple: give them homes.

Lesson: Find global solutions

In your own social enterprise journey, take the time to understand the global trends in the issue you are working to address. Where are the numbers going in the right direction and where are they going in the wrong direction? If you can understand the reasons why other countries are successfully tackling the issue you care about, then this can give you the inspiration to create a successful intervention in your area.

Putting it into practice

1. The key lesson from this experience in my life is the importance of researching best practice for tackling the issue you care about. In our case, in a world where the homelessness statistics are going in the wrong direction, we had to find the one place where numbers were reducing and understand the reasons why. When you are working to solve a social problem, others are always keen to share their learnings and tell you what has worked. It is different from the private sector where ideas are copyrighted and you cannot copy others' innovations. In the world of social entrepreneurship, ideas are shared and replicated in the hope of helping as many people as possible. So, don't feel the need to reinvent the wheel. Find out what is working and try to create a project to implement it in your area. If you do come up with an innovative intervention to your issue, be sure to share your learnings with others too.

2. The other critical takeaway from this experience is the importance of lobbying to change government policy on an issue. In my view, the holy grail of social entrepreneurship is to create a

project that ultimately leads to a change in public policy. This will require you to do much of the heavy lifting to establish the programme and sometimes a great deal of patience with government bureaucracy, as things in government naturally move slower than in an entrepreneurial environment. Don't get disheartened and keep your eye on the prize; achieving policy change is ultimately what is required if a social challenge is to be solved for good.

3. Collaboration is key. The Housing First programme that we catalysed became an incredible coalition of organisations over time. Five local councils were on board to pilot the programme and around 20 housing associations pledged homes. Fifteen local homelessness charities were commissioned across the five cities to deliver the support and Social Bite teamed up with the Scottish Government and other leading third sector organisations called the Corra Foundation and Homeless Network Scotland to oversee the programme. All of these organisations were expertly pulled together and chaired by Sir Andrew Cubie, who I had asked to play a vital convening role in the project (Andrew is also the current outstanding chair of Social Bite's parent charity). It was truly a collaborative effort to bring this to life and it was only through that collaboration that lasting change was achieved.

Chapter 13
Help just one person

Dode's Story – The power of Housing First

As much as it is important to try and bring about policy change, sometimes there is nothing more important than trying to help just one person. Changing just one person's life is within all of our power. In doing so, you can create a butterfly effect of change. The butterfly effect is the idea that small things can have non-linear impacts on a complex system. The concept is imagined with a butterfly flapping its wings, causing a chain of events which ultimately led to a typhoon. In the same way, by helping just one person, you can start to bring about much wider change.

To illustrate the power of this butterfly effect, as well as how Housing First works in practice for just one person, I wanted to tell you a story of the first person that was housed through our programme in Scotland, a man called Dode.

Paying it Forward

It was December 2017, one week prior to our Sleep in the Park event, and the STV 6 o'clock news had asked me if I would accompany one of their journalists to talk with rough sleepers in the centre of Edinburgh so that they could do a news story on the issue, as well as highlighting our upcoming event.

On this cold winter's night, I set off with a journalist called Kaye Nicolson and a cameraman around the streets of Edinburgh to meet and speak to various people sleeping rough – seeing if they might be prepared to talk about their story and their situation on camera. We wandered around for a couple of hours and met around six people who were bedding down in different doorways and alleyways. They each told their own emotional story on film, but the last person we met had a particularly harrowing life story. This man, in his mid-fifties, fragile, shivering and looking malnourished, sat in a doorway on Lothian Road in Edinburgh. He introduced himself as 'Dode'. Dode told the journalist his story on film and his interview was screened the following night on the 6 o'clock news.

Dode explained that he had been living on the streets of Edinburgh for 20 years, sleeping in doorways and often finding a place to sleep in the local graveyard. Dode had never had his own home before; the closest he had come was living in a squat in an abandoned property. He talked about how he had been bitten by a rat while sleeping on the street and had an infection in his legs. He showed the camera his infected legs and explained that he could barely walk.

He also said that he had a long-term alcohol addiction and a heroin addiction. He told us that he was HIV positive. He then looked down the camera lens and said, with a tear in his eye, 'If I am not indoors this winter, I will be dead.' He added heartbreakingly, 'People like me don't get second chances.'

Dode's interview aired on the STV 6 o'clock news. It was an extremely hard-hitting piece of journalism and Dode's story clearly affected the nation. We received an overwhelming number of emails and messages on social media asking us if we could just try to help this one man.

I knew we had been developing this Housing First programme to try to help rough sleepers into mainstream flats, but it was still several months away from being ready to launch officially. But given his desperate story and the fact that he said he was likely to die this winter on the street, I thought we had to at least try and do something. I thought maybe we could fast-track Dode into a house, give him the wrap-around support and he could be the first tenant in our Housing First programme. The following day, I phoned Martin Armstrong, the CEO of Scotland's largest housing provider, Wheatley Group. He had seen the piece on the news, so was already familiar with Dode's story. I asked Martin if he could provide a flat for Dode and we could pay to give him furniture and the comprehensive support he would need. Martin immediately agreed and asked his team to source a property.

With the flat secured, I decided to personally go to try and find Dode on the street to tell him the good news that we had managed to get him his own place alongside all of the support he was going to need. I went back to the same doorway on Lothian Road where we had found him a couple of nights prior – but it was empty. I wandered up and down the street searching in every doorway for him, but he was nowhere to be seen. I decided to speak to other rough sleepers in the area to see if they knew him. I met a younger man who was sitting in a sleeping bag, begging, outside of a Co-op shop. I said, 'I am looking for a man called Dode. I met him two nights ago when he spoke to a journalist for the television news. Since then he has been offered his own flat and I need to find him to tell him.' The young man knew exactly who Dode was. He told me that if I couldn't find him around the Lothian Road area he may be at the Royal Infirmary Hospital. He even knew which hospital ward Dode was likely to be in – the infections ward, ward 42. I asked if he knew Dode's real name to which he replied, 'George. George Riley.'

After thanking the young man, I phoned up the Edinburgh Royal Infirmary and asked to be put through to ward 42, and was immediately put through to a doctor on the ward. 'Hello, I was wondering if you had a patient called George Riley on your ward?' I asked. 'Yes, he's here,' the doctor replied. Brilliant! I was relieved to have tracked him down. I explained to the doctor the story of George being on the news and having been offered his own flat and I asked if I could come to visit him to tell him. The doctor asked George's permission and I arranged to go and see him the following day.

The next day, I arrived at ward 42 to find the man I had met freezing cold in a doorway three nights prior, looking fragile and lying in a gown on his hospital bed. He seemed very surprised to see me when I knocked on his door. I said to him, 'Remember that interview you did for the news a few nights ago? Well since then you have been offered your own permanent flat along with all of the support you might need to sustain it.' Dode burst into tears. He couldn't believe what I was telling him. 'What, my own flat? Permanently?' he asked. 'Yes,' I confirmed, nodding my head and smiling, the emotion of the moment hitting me. 'I cannot believe something good has come out of this,' he said, shaking his head in disbelief. 'I honestly thought I would be dead this winter,' he proclaimed, through more tears.

He was likely to be in hospital for several more weeks to deal with his leg infections, which gave us plenty of time to get his flat organised for him when he was discharged. I returned the following day to give him a mobile phone so that we could keep in touch with him and ensure that he didn't have to go back to the streets after he left hospital.

Several weeks later, Dode was picked up from hospital by his new support workers and taken to his new flat in the Gorgie area of Edinburgh. Basic furniture was already in place so it was already a lovely little flat for him to call his home – the first time he had been able to call somewhere home in his entire life. His newly assigned support workers started to visit him on a daily basis, offering the range of support that he needed.

Even though I had been publicly advocating for the adoption of this Housing First model in Scotland as a proven way to help long-term rough sleepers end their homelessness, I was worried that it might not work with Dode. In terms of complex needs, he ticked every single box:

- ✓ Severe physical health issues
- ✓ Severe mental health issues
- ✓ Lived on the streets for a long time (20 years)
- ✓ Alcohol addiction

Paying it Forward

✓ Heroin addiction
✓ No bank account
✓ Had never had his own flat before
✓ Never paid rent before
✓ Never had a job
✓ Never cooked for himself

Even after Dode had moved in, many questions ran through my mind. Was this going to work? Would there be trouble with the neighbours? How would he cope with suddenly having his own place? Could he hold down paying his rent? Would he get evicted before long?

After three weeks of him living in his new home, I decided to go and visit him to see how he was getting on. My worries were only compounded when I saw him. He told me he wasn't coping very well with the flat. He had not slept in a bed in over 20 years, so he had been sleeping on the living room floor rather than in his bed. He wasn't used to being enclosed by four walls. He was having withdrawal symptoms from alcohol and drugs and he was lonely living by himself. My heart broke when he told me he wanted to go back to the streets. Nevertheless, I encouraged him to stick with it. He was engaging well with his new support workers and seemed to appreciate them checking in on him on a daily basis, so I encouraged him to keep leaning on them and to give it some more time. I left Dode's flat that day very pessimistic about the likelihood he would remain there and not return to the street. I questioned whether this Housing First model that I had been lobbying the government to introduce could really work for someone with as many challenges as Dode.

Help just one person

Six months passed and my assumption was that Dode had probably left or been evicted by that stage. I decided to tentatively check whether he was still in the flat, and to my surprise, he was. I arranged another visit to see Dode in his home and I was amazed at what I saw. He welcomed me at his front door looking like a different person. Thanks to his support workers, he had been taking his medication properly and was looking much healthier physically. He had been eating regularly so he had put on some weight and was no longer the gaunt skeletal figure I had encountered on the street. He had begun to cherish the flat and showed me that he had painted the walls and bought some new furniture. He was taking great pride in his property. He had started sleeping in the bed. And he had stopped taking heroin. It was a truly remarkable transformation. I enquired with him what kind of support he had been receiving and he told me it was mainly simple things – the support workers would come each day and play cards with him, watch some television with him, check that he had food in the fridge, make sure he was keeping his doctor's appointments, taking his medication, claiming his benefits and keeping up with his rent.

I was blown away. This man had been living on the streets for 20 years. He faced every challenge you could imagine in physical health, mental health and addiction issues. No service had managed to break his cycle of homelessness for his whole adult life. He had been living through a constant revolving door of street living, prison and hospital admission, seemingly with no solution. And something as simple as giving him a house and some very basic support was all that was needed to break that lifelong cycle. It really wasn't rocket science. I am delighted to say that at the time of writing this, almost three years later, Dode is still happily living in his flat and doesn't seem likely to return to the streets ever again.

Dode's story made me more convinced by the model of Housing First than ever. If it can work for him, it can honestly work for anyone. I am thrilled that Dode's story has been replicated over a thousand times through our programme in Scotland and will be many times again as Housing First becomes our government's national policy to tackle homelessness.

Help just one person

Lesson: Help just one person

Sometimes social entrepreneurs can be too focused on 'changing the world', when in reality everything starts with helping just one person. Whether it was offering Pete a job in the cafe, or finding Dode a home, these solitary acts became our foundation for wider change.

Changing just one person's life is within all of our gift. So, look out for that one person in your life who might be suffering and use what you can to help them. You never know what butterfly effect you might help to create.

Putting it into practice

1. Remember the butterfly effect

A butterfly can flutter its wing leading to a chain of events that ultimately causes a typhoon. Don't get daunted by the scale of the social challenge you are trying to address, try and help just one person and you will be amazed at the wider change that might stem from that.

2. Never write anyone off

When I met Dode, it seemed like an impossible thing to do to get him off the streets. After all, he had been homeless for 20 years and nothing had worked. But that clearly says more about the broken system than it does about Dode – a simple solution of a mainstream home and simple support broke a lifelong cycle of homelessness.

3. Be patient for change

After 20 years of homelessness, when Dode first moved into his flat, he could not cope with it and wanted to move back to the streets. But some gentle encouragement and support from his workers was all he needed to make a remarkable transformation in his life.

Chapter 14
Impossible is nothing

Shutting down Times Square

In life, you will often be told that something is 'impossible' to do. This is a particularly British trait, where the general attitude can sometimes be somewhat pessimistic. Always remember that people say something is 'impossible' because it might seem so to them at that time. Almost every technological advancement was believed, at one point, to be impossible. But impossibility exists only when we believe it does. Sometimes we think of things as impossible only because we're underestimating our cognitive and physical abilities. We create impossibilities: we limit ourselves to what we believe we can accomplish and by doing so, we guarantee the change we're dreaming of never manages to arrive. I hope that this story from my life will inspire you to understand that, in the words of Muhammad Ali, 'impossible is nothing'. It also serves to demonstrate that you should not always take 'no' for an answer and that we all have the power to achieve whatever we set our minds to.

The success of our 'sleep out' events in Scotland, which grew from 270 people taking part in the 'CEO Sleepout' all the way to a nationwide mass participation event, had caused me wonder just how far we could push the boundaries. In 2018, we expanded the sleep outs to four Scottish cities, and the events raised over £8 million over a three-year period in Scotland and caused a wave of momentum and political urgency in tackling the issue. The problem with entrepreneurship is that it is addictive: after one success you want a bigger hit. I started to wonder if our vision was too narrow in focusing on homelessness purely in Scotland. Could we broaden our horizons and try to mobilise action on a global stage?

I thought back to my teenage years when my brother, Jack, won tickets for us to go to Sir Bob Geldof's Live 8 concert in Hyde Park, which was part of a global series of concerts to campaign against poverty. I thought about the time when my whole family, including my gran, marched on Richard Curtis's Make Poverty History march. Participating in these campaigns as a teenager planted a deep-rooted seed within me and I thought about how we could develop our sleep out concept into an international campaign.

Homelessness is a global issue, not a local one. As I outlined earlier in this book, even in the world's most affluent and developed economies, the issue of homelessness is getting worse. I decided therefore to try and create my very own 'Live 8' moment for the global homelessness issue and came up with an event campaign called 'The World's Big Sleep Out', taking inspiration from the previous events that I had organised, but raising the ambition to a global stage. I started to map out the goals and objectives of the campaign: we would try to convince 50 cities from all over the world to host simultaneous sleep out events. Each event would take palace on the same night and begin with a concert featuring performances from major, world-renowned acts, after which the participants would sleep out together, in unison with others all over the planet. I set a target of attracting 50,000 participants in every corner of the world, with the aim being to shine a global spotlight on the global issue of homelessness.

Given that I had never worked anywhere outside my home country of Scotland in the past, looking back I have no idea where the belief that this could even be possible came from. But I had years of experience in visualising ideas and being able to bring them to life. This vision was clearly more daunting, but I figured that the process of manifesting the idea into reality would be the same. In my mind, I could clearly see the end point of the campaign: a night of global solidarity with tens of thousands of people sleeping out in unison and millions of pounds raised. I could visualise this so clearly, in the same way as I had done with previous events that we had organised. This clear vision and sense of inner confidence propelled me to embark on what would be the most scarily ambitious project of my life.

In order to try and get 50 cities on board, I thought it would be critical to secure some iconic and high-profile locations to stage our major sleep out events. I had an aspiration to secure renowned venues in London and New York to host our flagship events: there we could host major concerts and have thousands of people bedding down for the night. As I said, I had only really worked in Scotland over the course of my career, and although I had developed an amazing network locally, I didn't have many connections outside my home country. I knew very few people in London and I didn't know anyone at all in New York.

One evening in late 2018, I decided to get started. Not sure where to start, I thought I would try and phone up the New York City Parks Department to enquire about securing one of their parks for the event. I was sitting on my sofa in my small flat in Edinburgh and googled 'New York Park Permitting' to try and find a phone number. I managed to locate the contact number for the permitting department for all of New York's parks and decided to simply cold-call them. *Here goes nothing*, I thought. I dialled the number and managed to get through to someone senior in that department called Will. I told Will all about our 'Sleep in the Park' events in Edinburgh with thousands of people sleeping out and millions of pounds raised. I explained that we wanted to stage a global campaign and we were looking for an iconic park in New York to host a major event. I was mid-flow when Will cut me off: 'I am sorry to interrupt you, Josh, but that will be impossible to do in New York,' he said. He went on to tell me that there was no precedent for overnight events in New York as all of the parks had a time curfew of 11pm. He said that there was no way that the NYPD would agree to an event like that and that his department would definitely not grant a permit. He concluded by informing me that if I ever wanted to do anything like this in New York, then I would really have to get the mayor on board and suggested I should try a different city. I hung up the phone somewhat deflated. It felt like the dream was over before it had even begun. But the next day I decided to persevere. I decided to book some flights out to New York for a few days to see if I could get any further in person.

Before I travelled out to New York, I wanted to set up as many meetings there as I could in order to make the most of my trip and try to secure a venue. There is an organisation in Scotland called 'The Global Scots' network, which is an association of people from all over the world with a Scottish heritage. In some cases, the members are Scottish themselves, but in most cases, it is people with a Scottish great-grandmother or some distant relative that gave them a Scottish connection, but in all cases, they have a strong affinity with Scotland. I met up with the coordinator of this network and asked for as many introductions as they could make for me with their members in New York. They got to work, and with around ten very random and speculative meetings in the diary, I flew off to New York to try to make something happen.

I arrived in New York at JFK airport and got a taxi into town. I had never been to New York before and the scale and vibrancy of this iconic city immediately hit me. It felt like stepping on to a movie set as I walked past endless skyscrapers and the dazzling billboards of Times Square to find my hotel. I suddenly felt like a very small fish in a very big pond.

Over the course of the next two days, I bounced around Manhattan on the subway and in taxis meeting the various people, all with a connection to Scotland, that I had been introduced to.

Paying it Forward

The meetings were all very speculative with a range of people from many backgrounds who had made New York their home. I was hoping to meet someone with political connections to try to overturn the long-standing status quo in New York of not granting permits for overnight events. In every meeting, I told the story of Social Bite, starting from the origins of our small cafe where a young man who was homeless had come in and asked us for a job. I shared the narrative of how we grew the organisation, built the village and I showed everyone a video of the original 'Sleep in the Park' event in Edinburgh where they could see the footage of 8,000 people bedding down on the coldest night of the year. I then went on to explain that we wanted to replicate this sleep out concept all over the world on one special night and we were looking for a venue in New York to host the flagship event.

Most of the meetings were fairly pointless and didn't really help me on my quest. But on my second day, I met with a property developer called Etai Gross. The Gross family were affluent real estate developers who owned several hotels in the city. When I showed Etai the Sleep in the Park video, he said to me, 'Josh, I am a bit of an introvert and I don't have many people in my network. But you should maybe meet my friend, Bruce – he might be able to help you.' I didn't have any idea who Bruce was, and Etai didn't elaborate, but I was keen to follow wherever the path led over the course of my three days in New York. Etai phoned his friend Bruce and set up a meeting for me the following day.

The next day I took a taxi to Bruce's office for the meeting. I still had no idea who Bruce was or the details of his background, but off I went to tell my story and show him the video of what we had done in Edinburgh. I arrived to meet Bruce, who was an extremely energetic and quite aggressive New Yorker. Fast talking – every second word was 'fuck' – he seemed like he was having a very busy day and that he had taken this meeting with me only as a bit of a favour to his friend Etai. I decided to ask Bruce his background, and much to my surprise he told me that he was the former chief of staff to Mayor Rudy Giuliani and that he was still very connected politically. Excited by having made such a potentially useful connection, I proceeded to tell Bruce the story of Social Bite starting from the cafe eight years earlier leading to me sitting in front of him this day. Bruce looked at me impatiently and then looked at his watch: 'I don't have all day, Josh,' he said abruptly. 'Get to the point.'

Slightly flustered and not used to the direct New York style, I decided to cut to the chase, showed him the video of the sleep out event from Edinburgh and explained that this was what we wanted to do in New York. As Bruce watched the video of thousands of people sleeping out in the freezing cold in Edinburgh and saw how much money was raised, he started to nod and smile. 'I fuckin' love this,' he muttered. When the three-minute video ended, Bruce burst into life: 'Josh, this is fuckin' great. We HAVE to do this in New York. New Yorkers will fuckin' love this and homelessness is such a fuckin' problem in the city right now,' he exclaimed. 'Do you know what?' he mused, 'I am going to phone someone in City Hall right now.' Bruce proceeded to pull out his mobile phone and make a call right there in front of me. 'Hello, Jason?' he barked down the phone, having obviously got through to a contact of his in the current mayor's office. 'Look, I am with this guy Josh from Scotland – you have got to give this guy ten minutes tomorrow about this "homeless thing", OK?' After a short back and forth, Bruce hung up the phone and said, 'OK, you have a meeting tomorrow in City Hall at 1pm.' He gave me his card and told me to phone him to tell him how I got on.

The following day I arrived at City Hall – a grand building in downtown New York where the mayor and other senior polit-ical figures are based. I was due to fly back to Scotland later that day, so I arrived at City Hall somewhat flustered, with my suitcase in hand. I checked in, through a tight security process, and went to meet with 'Jason' and two senior people in Mayor de Blasio's office. It turned out that Jason was in fact Jason Goldman, who was the chief of staff to another senior politi-cal figure, Corey Johnson, and had significant influence in the political word of New York City. By this time, I had got used to pitching the event, so I went through the same process of telling my story and showing the same video that had inspired Bruce to set up the meeting. I got a similar reaction: 'Josh, this is a really great idea,' they all concurred, all nodding enthusiastically in approval. I explained to them that I had phoned the permit-ting office in the New York City Parks Department and they had told me that there was no precedent for overnight events and that it would be 'impossible' for them to grant a permit for an event like this. 'Yes, that is true,' Jason Goldman said, 'that this would be very difficult to do in New York.' My heart sank, bracing myself for the potential of arriving at a dead end in my quest for a venue in New York for our sleep out. Jason went on,

Impossible is nothing

'But . . . I don't know . . . maybe, a venue that might work for this . . . might be . . . Times Square?' Times Square is one of the most iconic locations in the world; it is often referred to as 'the centre of the universe'. It is literally the world's most vis-ited tourist attraction, drawing an estimated 50 million visitors annually. Approximately 460,000 people pass through Times Square every single day. The only time in the year that Times Square is fully closed down for an event is for the Ball Drop on New Year's Eve. 'Erm . . .' I stuttered, 'that would work.'

Later that day I flew home to Scotland, amazed that my hand-ful of speculative meetings had led me all the way to the mayor's office and we were talking about closing down one of the world's most iconic locations. I wanted to strike while the iron was hot, so I arranged to travel back to New York a few weeks later to try and set up follow-up meetings and see if I could turn this suggestion into a reality. I returned to New York, but this time I had meetings set up with all of the key organisations that would be involved in giving the green light to a major event like this. I hopped around Manhattan to meet with the NYPD, the Times Square Alliance (who are the governing body of Times Square), the mayor's per-mitting team and New York's Homelessness Department. I did my usual pitch, by this stage on auto-pilot. I told them that Jason Goldman had suggested that Times Square might be a possible venue. Given that I had been told that this would be 'impossible' to do in New York – let alone in Times Square – I was expecting one of these meetings to present us with a roadblock. But each group of people that I met responded positively. Alongside their direct approach, New Yorkers have a 'can do' attitude and they loved the underdog story of a small cafe in Scotland bringing our campaign all the way to Times Square in New York. When we met with the Times Square Alliance, their lead event planner, Damian Santucci, started to bring out floor plans of the Times Square plazas and talk logistics. *Could this actually happen?* I thought. Suddenly 'impossible' didn't seem so impossible after all.

I left New York excited by the positive response I had received from everyone. We continued to correspond with the different departments over email and phone for several weeks, answering all of their questions and trying to ease any concerns. Just before Christmas 2018, I got a phone call from the mayor's office in New York: we had the green light. We had permission to close down all four plazas of Times Square on Saturday, 7 December 2019, to have over 1,000 people sleep out to raise funds and global awareness in a bid to tackle homelessness. I couldn't quite believe it: we were going to close down 'the centre of the universe' to shine a light on the plight of people who are so often ignored and made to feel invisible.

With Times Square in my back pocket, I decided to approach the office of the mayor of London, Sadiq Khan. I managed to arrange a meeting with the deputy mayor, James Murray, alongside one of the UK's most prominent homelessness experts, Dame Louise Casey, who couldn't have been more supportive of the planned campaign. I explained our plans to the deputy mayor and Dame Louise and told them that we were looking for an iconic venue in London for Saturday, 7 December. With Times Square confirmed it made their decision easy, and they offered us Trafalgar Square on the spot. I was thrilled. We now had two of the world's most iconic locations confirmed and it was game on. With these venues, I was confident that we could raise global awareness of an issue that I had been passionate about ever since we had offered Pete that job eight years earlier. For one night, we were going to make *our* issue, *the world's* issue.

Paying it Forward

Lesson: Impossible is nothing

When you are setting out on your own entrepreneurial path, you will often be told that something is 'impossible' or 'can't be done'. This experience shows beyond doubt what the great late boxer Muhammad Ali said is true: 'Impossible is just a big word thrown around by small men who find it easier to live in the world they've been given than to explore the power they have to change it. Impossible is not a fact. It's an opinion. Impossible is not a declaration. It's a dare. Impossible is potential. Impossible is temporary. Impossible is nothing.'

Putting it into practice

1. When you really believe in something and you believe in yourself, don't take 'no' for an answer, at least not straight away. Keep knocking on the door, because you never know what might lie behind it.

2. There are only six degrees of separation between you and any other person on the planet. Think about that for a second. You are only six introductions away from the president of the United States or anyone else on earth for that matter. To make my vision happen, I had to somehow make my way into the mayor of New York's office. That might seem unrealistic, but it actually only took me three introductions to do so. And I had never met anyone from New York before in my life! So, don't be afraid to get out there and meet people, tell them your vision and ask for an introduction if you need one. Network until you find the person that you need to help you. They can only ever be six introductions away.

3. Dream big. I could never have believed we would have secured Times Square as a venue for our event and it was an incredible experience to see that become a reality. So aim for the stars – you never know what is possible until you try.

Chapter 15
Build a movement

Will Smith and The World's Big Sleep Out

On your own social entrepreneurship journey, you will be immersed in creating a project that tackles a social issue you care about. This can often feel very lonely as you get bogged down with a range of challenges and problems that will inevitably come your way. But remember that there are likely to be thousands of people all over the world who also care passionately about the same social issue as you. As well as creating a social enterprise or charity, you have the opportunity to build a movement of like-minded people all uniting to drive positive change. You have the chance to amplify your voice and shine a light on the issue you care about by bringing people together who care about the cause.

Recent movements that have driven positive change include Black Lives Matter, School Strike for Climate, Girls' Right to Education and the #MeToo movement. By bringing people together behind a particular issue, these movements have managed to accelerate the pace of social change like never before. The advent of social media has enabled movements to spread globally at a rate never before seen in history. From documenting and sharing images and videos of police violence, to inciting legislative changes from local leaders, social media's role in prompting and sustaining social movements cannot be understated. So, in your social entrepreneurship adventure, give some thought to how you might unite people behind your cause and create a movement for change.

My experience of the homelessness issue had always only been at a very local level in my own country. But I was becoming increasingly aware of the global nature of the challenge. The United Nations Human Settlements Programme estimates that, throughout the world, 1.6 billion people live in inadequate housing, and the best data available suggests that more than 100 million people globally have no housing at all. There are an estimated 70.8 million people displaced throughout the world because of war, natural disasters and extreme poverty. Street homelessness affects people in every region of the world – developed and developing – and in the absence of coordinated global action, it is growing. The imbalance between supply and demand of housing, displacement driven by political and economic causes, and the lack of a safety net for the most vulnerable all contribute to the growth of street homelessness. As the Institute of Global Homelessness highlights, this is one of the great and visible social ills of our time, and yet there has been no coordinated global response to tackle it on a par with other issues related to poverty and health.

Build a movement

With Times Square and Trafalgar Square secured as venues for our events, I was sure that we could create a campaign that would bring global attention to this global challenge. I was confident that we could create our very own 'Live Aid' moment for the global homelessness issue. I wanted to raise a substantial sum of money for charities tackling the issue all over the world and also to try and move the dial politically.

We set an objective of securing at least 50 cities to host major sleep out events all over the world on the same night. The goal was for each event to have a concert featuring prominent musicians and a famous actor telling a 'bedtime story' to participants before they slept out for the night, like we had done with Liam Gallagher and John Cleese in Edinburgh. We were hoping that we could find 50,000 people to participate in sleeping out all over the world, in solidarity with people who were homeless and that didn't have a choice. We would encourage each participant to fundraise and I hoped that we could raise millions of pounds to benefit local homelessness charities all over the world.

This was by far the most challenging and daunting thing I had ever undertaken in my life, but I had got so used to seeing my ideas become a reality, that I was approaching it with a mindset of absolute certainty. I was sure we could pull it off.

Staging a major global campaign is not a cheap endeavour, so one of the first things we had to do was source some funding to allow us to begin covering the costs of putting this on. A few years earlier, I had met a prominent businessman and philanthropist in Edinburgh called Hamid Guedroudj, who is the founder of a major software engineering company called Petex. Hamid is a hyper-intelligent and larger-than-life character, whom I had met with his wife Faiza at a business function. I met them both after I had consumed a bit too much to drink. I was drunkenly smoking a cigarette outside the venue and got chatting to Hamid who was also smoking and we immediately hit it off. Ever since that seren-dipitous meeting, Hamid has always been one of our most generous supporters and he is always the first person I would go to with a new idea to pitch for his backing. He also opened my eyes to a wider definition of homelessness, educating me on the plight of refugees and displaced children all over the world, an issue that is very close to his heart. With my new-found aspirations to 'go global', I went to meet Hamid and his financial controller, Lynn, at their office in Edinburgh to tell them about my ambitious plan and to ask for a donation to help us recruit a team and cover some of the budgeted costs of putting on this major global endeavour. Despite the fact that I had no real experience or credibility to make this massive leap in staging an international event, Hamid has always had a great deal of faith in me, and decided to back the plan. He offered a major donation to help us cover our costs. I will always be immensely grateful to Hamid for his incredible generosity. Occasionally in life, we all meet people that will back us. When we meet these people, we must cherish them, as they make the difference in all acts of cre-ation. Without Hamid's support, the reality is that I would never have been able to get this plan, as well as many plans before it, off the ground.

With Hamid's funding in place, alongside further support from a range of corporate sponsors, we started to invest in the key elements of staging our flagship events and to recruit a team to help make this vision a reality. We hired a team of four multilingual people – Erin, Eduardo, Maria and Marion – to start reaching out to cities all over the world. Their job was to approach various city governments to try and persuade them to join the campaign by hosting an official sleep out event on Saturday, 7 December 2019. We also recruited a central logistics team alongside a team of two fundraisers in New York and two fundraisers in London, whose remit was to engage the business community to have employees sleeping out and fund-raising at the events. My colleague Jamie Boyd, who started with Social Bite as a van driver delivering sandwiches some years earlier, was put in charge of all of the operations and logistics for this global campaign. When I looked at all of the new team members for this campaign, absolutely none of them, including me, had ever had any experience of putting on an international fundraising campaign. It was a group of young, motivated and somewhat off-beat people who had bought into my vision and believed that together we could change the world.

We also put together a board of trustees to govern the campaign and Dame Louise Casey agreed to chair. In 1997, Dame Louise became Tony Blair's homelessness 'tsar' and presided over policies that reduced the number of people who were homeless in the UK by two thirds over a decade. Dame Louise had watched on in horror as the homelessness statistics gradually got worse under consecutive Conservative governments from 2007 until the present day when the numbers of people sleeping rough on our streets are now higher than ever. This was a point of great personal anguish for Louise so she threw herself into our campaign with great vigour and passion.

Paying it Forward

With most of the team recruited by February 2019, we were planning on launching the campaign to the public, globally, a few months later in May. Time wasn't our side, so in order to try to engage as many cities as possible to host events, we compiled a database of every single mayor in every major city in the world – and we wrote every single one a letter inviting them to become a host city. Our multilingual city outreach team then followed up with each city to try and secure as many events as possible. With New York and London already on board, the strategy started to pay off and cities started to come back to us to get involved in the campaign. The first to confirm were all in the UK – Cardiff, Belfast, Dublin, Edinburgh and Newcastle. As the month passed, the snowball grew and more cities started to confirm sleep out events, including Chicago, Santiago in Chile, New Delhi in India, Brisbane in Australia, Madrid in Spain, Manila in the Philippines and Hong Kong. All of these cities were grappling with their own homelessness issue and saw the campaign as a way to raise awareness and much-needed funds. I was thrilled that things were starting to come together and that we had managed to secure cities from every corner of the globe.

The big public launch in May was fast approaching and in order to engage the public to participate I really wanted to secure some high-profile musicians to perform and A-list celebrities to tell the bedtime stories. If you think about any successful mass participation fundraising campaign, such as Live Aid or Comic Relief, support from musicians and celebrities tends to be critical when generating significant awareness and funds – so I was determined to make this happen. I was thinking about what access we may have to the A-list world of celebrities and I thought back to George Clooney's visit to Social Bite in Scotland and wondered if he might be able to support or introduce me to some of his actor friends to get involved. I reached out to George's speaking agent Holly to explain what we had planned and said that I was looking for someone high profile to tell the bedtime story in Times Square, New York. She told me that George was filming a new movie over the date of the event and would not be available, but she said she would make some enquiries with other Hollywood actors to see if anyone might be able to get involved. A few days later I got a phone call from Holly telling me that she had someone that would be interested in participating – Will Smith. I couldn't believe it – Will Smith had been one of my favourite actors ever since he made *The Fresh Prince of Bel-Air*. In 2006, he had made a movie called *The Pursuit of Happyness* that told the story of Chris Gardner, a man who became homeless with his son in San Francisco, and Will had been passionate about the homelessness issue since then. Will Smith also had his own foundation called the Will and Jada Pinkett Smith Foundation which *focused* on tackling poverty and supporting marginalised communities, so we were able to get him on board in a similar way to how we had done with Clooney and DiCaprio: by offering some significant support to foundation as part of our events, with the support of corporate sponsors and philanthropic backers. I was confident Will's global stardom and social media following (which was in the tens of millions) would help us attract participants all over the world.

With Will Smith secured for telling a bedtime story to participants at the New York event, the final thing I felt it was important to secure prior to launching the campaign was a celebrity to be his counterpart in London. I was thinking about iconic actors in the UK and Dame Helen Mirren is undoubtedly a national treasure that I thought would be perfect. I simply googled 'Dame Helen Mirren' and found a website for her with an email address for her manager. I sent off a speculative email detailing our plans for the campaign, the fact that Will Smith was performing the bedtime story in New York and invited Dame Helen to do the same in London. After about two weeks of silence, a reply popped into my inbox saying that Dame Helen would be interested in supporting. I spoke with her manager, Sandy, on the phone and before long Dame Helen was also confirmed. With Will Smith, Dame Helen Mirren and various iconic cities all over the world on board so far, we were ready to launch The World's Big Sleep Out to the public.

The date of the launch was 8 May 2019. On the day, myself and our chair, Dame Louise Casey, had secured a spot on the sofa of one of the most watched chat shows in the UK – *The One Show* – to announce the campaign. We appeared on the sofa, next to Eric Stonestreet who plays Cameron in the TV show *Modern Family* to be interviewed about The World's Big Sleep Out. I told the host Matt Baker, along with the 6 million viewers at home, the story about how I had managed to secure Times Square as well as the history of Social Bite. I went on to announce that global superstars Will Smith and Dame Helen Mirren were signed on to tell the 'bedtime stories' and we were hoping to have 50,000 people sleeping out all over the world. I passionately implored the public watching at home to sign up to sleep out on 7 December for a global moment of compassion, and we directed everyone to the website. It was truly a fantastic opportunity to launch the campaign in such a high-profile way and we were officially up and running.

The next morning, I nervously asked Jamie how many sign-ups we had managed to generate from the launch. Our target was to find 50,000 people to sleep out all over the world, so I was really hoping that people in their thousands would have signed up after hearing about us on *The One Show*. Jamie told me that after the launch day, we only had around 1,000 registrations. Almost all of the initial participant sign-ups were in the UK, with very little in the other participating cities overseas. *Oh, God*, I thought, with a sense of déjà vu, *We have a very long way to go.*

As the weeks and months passed, I was under an increasing amount of pressure to pull everything together. We had so many hurdles still to clear to make this campaign a success. We still had to find another 40 cities to agree to become hosts and another 49,000 people to sleep out and raise funds! I was trying each day to keep faith in my belief that things would somehow conspire in our favour, but as each day passed I was becoming increasingly anxious about whether we would pull this off.

With the city sales team steadily recruiting new host cities, personally contacting mayors and city leaders, we were making a little bit of headway on growing the list of host cities that would stage sleep out events. We had now recruited fundraisers in ten cities all over the world, so for the first time in my life I was trying to manage a global team. I decided to focus my personal energies on trying to generate participation and fundraising in London and New York – where we were hoping to raise the majority of the funds. The campaign was my vision and nobody could pitch for support with more passion and authenticity than me, so my view was that I physically needed to be where the money was. I travelled back and forth to London on a weekly basis to seek support. The majority of major global companies we needed to pitch for support are headquartered in New York, so on that basis, I decided to travel to New York for six weeks, with six months to go until the date of the World's Big Sleep Out.

My objective for the trip was to try and personally engage corporate America in The World's Big Sleep Out. We had formed a partnership with UNICEF USA and I had been introduced to their CEO at the time, Caryl Stern, who is a powerful charity leader in America. Caryl decided to also throw her weight behind my vision and opened up her contact book for me in New York. With Caryl's introductions, I was able to get meetings with CEOs and senior leaders at companies such as JP Morgan, Unilever, WeightWatchers, Nasdaq, Deloitte, PWC and countless others. I told each person that we met the story of Pete asking us for a job in our cafe all the way to us securing Times Square. I asked them to get their company behind it and ask their employees to sleep out and raise funds. As I found to be the American way, the response I got almost every time was overwhelmingly positive: 'Josh – we LOVE this! We LOVE you! We are going to get right behind you and have our teams sleep out in Times Square and globally to raise funds! We will raise a fortune!' I had been used to pitching my ideas in Scotland where the typical initial response was often 'That'll never work!' So I couldn't believe how open and positive the culture was in America. Before long the president of the Nasdaq stock exchange, Adena Friedman, had agreed to sleep out in Times Square along with the CEOs of many of America's corporate titans. *Wow! America is easy!* I thought, suddenly feeling much more optimistic about our prospects of making the campaign a success.

I returned home to Scotland in mid-July feeling excited and energised by my six-week stint in New York. As time passed, that excitement turned into anxiety when we reached back out to all of the people that I had met. Many of the people that had given us such overwhelmingly glowing feedback had suddenly gone a bit quiet. Many of the people that were so unbelievably positive to me in person were not coming back to us to confirm participation numbers or to start fundraising. We were struggling to convert their initial positivity into concrete actions and the number of sign-ups were still much too slow. I wasn't sure if they had just told me to my face what I wanted to hear, but had no intention of following through, or whether they were just so busy that they were struggling to prioritise our campaign.

As the summer months passed and the date of The World's Big Sleep Out drew closer, my emotions were a real roller coaster. Each day seemed to bring amazing new opportunities but we were also really struggling to engage participants all over the world, we hadn't managed to secure any musicians to perform yet and we had so far raised almost nothing instead of the millions we had been hoping for. I had to consistently battle my internal dialogue to keep myself and the team positive and motivated. Rather than look at these massive goals and think about how far away we still were, we tried to just make progress and take it one day at a time. Rather than thinking about the massive wall we had to build, we sought to lay just one brick at a time. I was working every hour God sent, and my travel schedule was becoming increasingly intense. Slowly but surely new cities started to sign up – Los Angeles, Hutt City, Brighton, San Jose, Manchester, Wacken in Germany and Harare in Zimbabwe all came on board. As each new city signed up it gave me and the team a real boost to keep pushing on.

As we got closer to 7 December for the night of The World's Big Sleep Out, the campaign had completely taken over my life. I felt like I was living in an airport – constantly travelling to London or America or one of the other host cities to try and drum up more support. My stress levels were rising each day and I was constantly concerned that I had over-reached and bitten off more than I could chew. My panic attacks had returned. My mindset of absolute certainty had given way to one of consistent doubts and uncertainties. Would we be able to secure enough funds to put all of the events on? Would we raise any money at all? As my life became consumed by the effort required to make the campaign happen, I was growing increasingly distant from my friends and family. I hadn't phoned my mum in months. I felt like I was letting Sukhi down, as I wasn't able to give her the time or the love that she deserved. Even when I was with her physically, my mind was elsewhere, thinking about the million things I had to do, or I was engrossed in my laptop, replying to emails until late at night. Failure would have been catastrophic for me, but much more so for the thousands of people that we were aiming to support. The pressure was weighing heavily on my shoulders and I was struggling to carry it. I remember it all got too much one evening when I was sitting in London City airport awaiting a flight home to Edinburgh.

Build a movement

Sukhi phoned me, worried about how I was coping and I broke down in floods of tears in the middle of the airport over the phone. I had nothing left to give. I really was on the edge.

I confided in my dad about the intense pressure that I was under and my fear that the campaign could be a failure and the implications of this. He shared with me an extract from a speech made by Theodore Roosevelt that had helped him through times he'd felt under pressure. The speech, 'Citizenship in a Republic', had been given at the Sorbonne in Paris in April 1910, and the extract itself is known as the 'Man in the Arena'. Reading it made me well up with emotion and helped give me the strength I needed to keep pushing:

It is not the critic who counts: not the man who points out how the strong man stumbles, or where the doer of deeds could have done them better. The credit belongs to the man who is actually in the arena, whose face is marred by dust and sweat and blood, who strives valiantly, who errs and comes up short again and again, because there is no effort without error or shortcomings, but who knows the great enthusiasms, the great devotions; who spends himself in a worthy cause; who, at the best, knows, in the end, the triumph of high achievement, and who, at the worst, if he fails, at least he fails while daring greatly, so that his place shall never be with those cold and timid souls who knew neither victory nor defeat.

You've never lived until you've almost died. For those who have fought for it, life has a flavour the protected shall never know.

Paying it Forward

With the support of my incredible team, our big supporter Hamid, our chair, Dame Louise Casey, and all the other amazing people who started to get behind the effort, I mustered up all of my resolve, we kept the faith and kept pressing forward. And sure enough, in the final months, the little miracles I had been praying for started to happen. Mark Thompson, the CEO of one of the world's most influential newspapers, the *New York Times*, had heard about the campaign and offered to host a fundraising breakfast for us. Mark hosted the breakfast in the boardroom of the *New York Times* and invited many of New York's most influential leaders to support. The UK's former prime minister, Tony Blair, even attended to support the campaign. the *New York Times* wrote a major article about us, which resulted in people from all over the world signing up to participate and fundraise.

With six weeks to go until the big night, I was introduced to one of my campaigning heroes, Richard Curtis. I met Richard at his office in London to ask him for his support. As well as being an amazing movie director of films like *Love Actually* and *Notting Hill*, Richard is one of the world's best charity campaigners, founding Comic Relief and Make Poverty History. Richard's office is on Portobello Road in London, directly above the book shop that features in the *Notting Hill* movie. I told Richard how I had taken part in his Make Poverty History march as a child and how it had inspired me to do what I was now doing. Richard really understood the power of ambitious campaigns and what we were trying to achieve. He probably also saw the panic in my eyes and started listing the many ways he could support me. He immediately started to introduce me to other people who could help. One of the people

Build a movement

that Richard introduced me to was the CEO and chairman of Sony Music, Jason Iley, whom I met at short notice the following day. I told Jason about what we had planned and how we only had six weeks to make it happen, hoping that he could help us to secure A-list musicians to perform, which would really help us to engage the public in the campaign. Jason immediately got the vision, as well as the urgency, and he said he would reach out to all of Sony's artists all over the world. Within days, major music stars had started to confirm that they would perform live at the events. Ellie Goulding, Meghan Trainor, Rag'n'Bone Man, Travis, Tom Walker, Ziggy Marley, Jake Bugg, Gang of Youths, Frank Turner, The Script and many more all came on board to perform in cities throughout the world. I breathed a massive sigh of relief – this might just work!

I was also introduced to a Scotsman called David Dinsmore who is the chief operating officer of News International, Rupert Murdoch's media empire. When I met David and other senior editors at News International's glass skyscraper in London and pitched The World's Big Sleep Out, one person in the meeting said, 'I think we need to get Rebekah to call Rupert and get the tanks lined up behind this!' I felt like I was about to win an election!

Things got even harder to believe when just prior to The World's Big Sleep Out, the president of Nasdaq, Adena Friedman, invited me to ring the closing bell of the Nasdaq stock exchange. This surreal moment was beamed on to the massive Times Square billboard outside and was covered by all of the major business media.

With the support of the musicians and media coverage ramping up all over the world, people started to sign up to sleep out in their thousands. As well as signing up for the official events, thousands of people started to sign up to host their own sleep outs in their back gardens, high school playing fields or workplaces. Many of the companies I had pitched to months earlier started to come on board at the last minute. Will Smith shared details of the campaign to his 60 million Instagram and Facebook followers and thousands more people signed up to sleep out all over the world. Right when I needed it to, things started to come together.

We reached 7 December and I was filled with excitement, gratitude and, most of all, relief. By the night of the event, 52 cities had signed up to become official hosts and an incredible 60,000 people had signed up to sleep out in unison all over the world! I was blown away. All of the participants had been fundraising for local homelessness charities in their city as well as for child refugees throughout the world and in the final few days before the event the funds started to flood in. A major foundation called the OAK Foundation pledged to donate $1 million. Google donated $250,000. Facebook donated $400,000. Walgreens raised $550,000 from all of their stores in New York and California. Graeme Watt and Softcat raised almost $250,000 Unilever donated $50,000. A Dundee-based company called Insights Learning and Development donated $50,000, and an Edinburgh businessman called David Wither donated the same again. And 60,000 individuals in every corner of the planet were all raising as much as they could. By the time the night arrived, the campaign had generated almost $10 million! I was overwhelmed with emotion when I heard the final total.

I decided to spend the night sleeping out in Times Square in New York. My whole family – my mum, dad, brother, cousins and partner – all flew out to sleep out in New York too. On the day of The World's Big Sleep Out, the events management company built the stage and put barriers around the four plazas of Times Square. Before any participants had arrived, there was a moment when Sukhi and I stood alone in the middle of Times Square as it was closed down to the public. I took a deep breath and soaked it in – we had literally closed down 'the centre of the universe' for our cause. On the night, I had the privilege of introducing Will Smith on to the stage for his bedtime story. Will was fantastic with the audience and told everyone how important the cause was and how much he had learned about homelessness when filming *The Pursuit of Happyness*. Will then chose the theme tune to *The Fresh Prince of Bel-Air* as his bedtime story. After the show, I got into my sleeping bag in the middle of Times Square along with everyone else. I had been receiving updates from all 52 events throughout the world – due to time differences most of them had already happened and had all gone really well. The first events were in New Zealand and Australia and then went on throughout the world – the UK, India, the Philippines, Chicago and would finish in Los Angeles. Sukhi and I lay side by side in the middle of Times Square, holding hands, looking around at the bright billboard advertisements and the thousands of people bedding down alongside us, both absolutely overawed and relieved.

The World's Big Sleep Out was covered by every major media outlet throughout the world and brought massive awareness to the homelessness issue. The PR firms we were working with informed us that the total reach of the media coverage was an unbelievable 49,869,543,241! This global media coverage directly fed into a major lobbying effort on homelessness at the United Nations and in February 2020, I gave a speech at the United Nations in New York for the Commission on Social Development.

Under the leadership of the Institute of Global Homelessness, this lobbying effort resulted in the first UN resolution on homelessness in more than 30 years. The hope now is that this new focus on homelessness will play a key role in ensuring that 'no one is left behind' in the final decade of action towards the 2030 agenda for Sustainable Development Goals – and hopefully the world will find a way to put a roof over everyone's head.

Lesson: Build a movement (and keep the faith)

The World's Big Sleep Out campaign was undoubtedly the most stressful, scarily ambitious and all-consuming project I have ever undertaken and probably ever will. The project brought me to the absolute edge of my comfort zone and, in all honesty, I don't think that I would ever take such a major gamble again. It put an inordinate amount of stress not only on my own shoulders, but on all of the team, board members and supporters that worked so hard to make it happen. It is also the thing I am most proud of in my social entrepreneurship journey. I learned and grew as a person and a leader through overcoming the challenges that came my way. It also enabled Social Bite to grow to the next level as an organisation, gaining support from people all over the world. The campaign directly enabled Social Bite to open a cafe in London and has resulted in a range of funding opportunities and partnerships that have contributed millions of pounds in funding to the organisation since the event took place. So, in your journey, don't be afraid to push yourself almost to the point of failure – that is where the growth happens.

Putting it into practice

1. Uniting around a common purpose

This experience in my life taught me the importance of bringing people together from all walks of life to unite behind a common purpose. If the issue you care about is prevalent globally then it is possible to find like-minded supporters and advocates all over the world to unite behind your cause.

2. Keep the faith

In my experience, embarking on a mission like this can be immensely stressful, all-consuming and can take over your life. When it all starts to feel too much, try to keep the faith in your vision. The miracles you need will come, if you persevere.

3. If you fail, fail while daring greatly

When you go to the gym and do weights, your muscles will only grow if you lift weights to the point of fatigue; when your muscles are pushed to their limits. The World's Big Sleep Out campaign pushed me to my absolute limit mentally, and as the stress intensified, my fear that the campaign might fail became all-consuming in my mind. But it was only by pushing almost to breaking point that I was able to grow more as a person and as a leader, in an experience more challenging than any other in my career. The campaign also enabled our charity to move to the next level and establish support all over the world.

If the worst happens and you do fail, remember Theodore Roosevelt's words: 'For those who have had to fight for it, life has truly a flavour the protected shall never know.'

Chapter 16
A world turned upside down

I am currently writing this chapter as the world emerges from a string of lockdowns due to the global Covid-19 pandemic.

On 31 December 2019, the World Health Organization (WHO) was informed of a cluster of cases of pneumonia of an unknown cause, detected in Wuhan City, Hubei Province, China. On 9 January 2020, it was announced that a novel coronavirus had been identified in samples obtained from these cases and that initial analysis of virus genetic sequences suggested that this was the cause of the outbreak. This virus, and the associated disease of Covid-19, started to spread all over the world like wildfire resulting in a series of national lockdowns restricting freedom of movement and enforcing social distancing.

On Monday, 16 March 2020, life as we knew it was turned upside down when the UK's Prime Minister Boris Johnson announced a national lockdown. While this caused immense challenges for people from all walks of life, the lockdown also had particular implications for Social Bite. The general public was told not to visit cafes, bars and restaurants in order to limit the spread of the virus, so all of our cafes had to close overnight. As a social enterprise, more than 50 per cent of our total revenue came from our five cafes, our restaurant and our corporate catering business. All of a sudden that income had stopped without warning. While we were in the middle of an unprecedented health crisis, it was now clear that there was a parallel economic crisis to contend with. For Social Bite, along with the rest of the world's hospitality industry, it threatened our very existence.

The very next day, the senior leadership team and I had a crisis meeting. Of course, we were extremely concerned about the future of the charity we had spent nine years building. Much more importantly we were all very aware that the people we were helping every day would be the worst affected. For most of us, we could at least isolate in our homes, safe and secure with stocked up fridges and cupboards. Now imagine being homeless, having no home to self-isolate in. Furthermore, many of the support services that people who were homeless were relying on had been forced to close down. As much as we were concerned about the future of Social Bite, it simply wasn't an option to batten down the hatches and try to minimise the economic impact – we had to run into the fire in order to be there for the people who needed us at this most desperate time.

When news came in that Boris Johnson had contracted coronavirus, people started to say that the illness was a 'great leveller' – that it didn't matter what your position was in society, we were all equally susceptible – rich or poor. But this was simply not true. Those at the bottom of the socio-economic ladder were much more likely to contract the disease and be seriously economically impacted. Furthermore, the Covid-19 crisis was making social inequality even greater. Those on the front line of the pandemic were nurses, bus drivers, shelf stackers and care home workers – all disproportionately lower-paid members of society. They were all much more likely to catch the disease, because they were more exposed. Post-pandemic, many countries are experiencing recession and the World Trade Organization has warned that the world faces the deepest economic downturn of our lifetimes. As we emerged from the pandemic and into a cost of living crisis, the poorer members of society, many of whom have no savings or financial buffer, suffered, and are still suffering, severe consequences, the most extreme of which is finding themselves homeless. Indeed, many charities in the homelessness sector were bracing themselves for a significant increase in the people they were required to support. For those already in a situation of homelessness – who were either sleeping on our city's streets or in crowded homeless accommodations – the health risks of Covid-19 were stark and the economic downturn meant even more remote prospects of social mobility.

In those early days of the first lockdown, as we thought about the impact of the crisis on those at the bottom of the economic ladder, it became apparent to us that one of the biggest risks of the lockdown was widespread food poverty. People who were homeless would not be able to access many of the traditional food services that they may have previously relied on. Furthermore, there were thousands of families who were relying on free school meals that would no longer have access to them. There would be tens of thousands of hourly paid workers made redundant, with no savings in the bank and no immediate access to state benefits. To make matters worse, donations to food banks had fallen off a cliff as people were panic buying in supermarkets and keeping all of their non-perishable food supplies to themselves. I once heard that civilised society is only ever nine meals away from anarchy. If our society was to get through this lockdown in one piece, it was absolutely critical that the widespread food poverty that would emerge was addressed.

With this in mind, we wanted Social Bite to play our part. We very quickly decided to repurpose the focus of our entire organisation for the duration of the Covid-19 crisis. Our cafes, our restaurant, our central production kitchen, our vans and drivers were all at a standstill as we were effectively closed for business. We decided that we would redeploy our entire infrastructure to create a major free food delivery service for people who were homeless and other vulnerable groups. Our plan was to produce thousands of emergency food packs consisting of a freshly made sandwich, piece of fruit, packet of crisps and a drink. Within three days, on Friday, 20 March, the first 600 food packs were produced and delivered to people through our network of cafes, but we knew that this was only scratching the surface of need.

In order to reach as many people as possible, our team started to phone up charities and grass-roots community groups across Scotland offering them free food, if they could distribute it to those in need. Quickly word spread about this offer and many organisations started reaching out to us every day to request more food. It was clear that the level of need out there was significant and growing every day as the crisis deepened. Our incredible team rose to the challenge as 15 staff in our central kitchen worked ten hours per day to produce the food needed to keep up the demand. I will always be grateful to our team for putting themselves on the front line every day to meet this vital need.

As we emerged from the pandemic, Social Bite were able to deliver over 800,000 food packs through a series of national lockdowns. These have reached people who are homeless, hungry families and many others who would have found themselves in severe food poverty. This scale of production made the service the largest free freshly made food distribution programme in the UK at the time. As I have come to expect, the public, the business community and the Scottish Government once again rallied behind us, creating another clear moment in my life of incredible collaboration and collective compassion as they helped us achieve that level of food distribution. An incredible £2 million was donated to Social Bite over the course of the lockdowns to help us meet the demand and we came out of the other side of the crisis strong and ready to serve. One of the great silver linings to come out of the Covid-19 crisis was the clear sense of community spirit that emerged.

A new dawn

Within almost two years, by January 2022, there were 311,314,799 reported cases of Covid-19 across 185 countries and territories, and 5,514,602 deaths.

The unforeseen global health challenge created by the pandemic had brought the world to a standstill. Saving lives became the primary and most critical issue in every corner of the globe. This unprecedented moment in time challenged each of us in ways we did not think possible. During the lockdowns, while confined I was able to step off the treadmill of my life for a while. I had more time than usual to reflect on the past and think more deeply about the future. I am sure many of us felt this time was an unusual opportunity for reflection.

The pandemic in many ways put the world as we knew it on pause. The question is, do we want to simply continue where we left off now that things have supposedly resumed to normality? Or did the pandemic give us a chance, as a society and as a world, to look back at where the systems we created have failed us, and to consider how we might reinvent ourselves? Has the pandemic presented us with a collective opportunity, in the wake of devastation, to build a new socio-economic system? Or will we simply revert to business as usual?

Because, while 'business as usual' has delivered much prosperity and advancement for the world, it has also led to the following reality:

- The world's richest 1 per cent have more than twice as much wealth as **6.9 billion people combined**
- Almost half of humanity is living on **$5.50 a day**
- Today, 258 million children – **one out of every five** – will not go to school
- **Every day, 10,000 people die** because they **lack access to affordable healthcare**
- Each year, **100 million people are forced into extreme poverty because of healthcare costs.**

I believe that this crisis has given us the opportunity to think about how we can create a world where no one is left behind. During the pandemic, my own personal hero, Professor Muhammad Yunus, wrote a letter to the social business community arguing that, 'The spread of this illness serves to highlight beyond doubt how interconnected we all are. We must build a system where each one is recognised as a part of the whole. Nobody is an island, no matter how rich and powerful. The complete system of life is not limited to human beings alone; the system includes all life forms and the natural world that makes up our planet. It has never been as clear as it is today that interconnectivity has turned the whole world into a small neighbourhood. No one is unknown; no one is too far from anyone else.'

Now that the world has emerged from Covid-19 and returned to a sense of normality, there is no way that we can ignore the severe deprivation that we see in our communities; we cannot say that it is not our problem. The pandemic has demonstrated beyond doubt that our lives are interconnected and intertwined.

We are at a moment of human restructuring. These moments happen very occasionally in human history, whether it was the creation of our National Health Service (NHS) and welfare state after the Second World War; the dawning of the digital age, where we began to understand our world through the device in our pocket; or the post-Cold War hegemony of the capitalist ideology as the best way to advance human prosperity. In this moment, having emerged from the global pandemic, it's all up for grabs.

Arundhati Roy summed it up when writing for the *Financial Times*: 'Historically, pandemics have forced humans to break with the past and imagine their world anew. This one is no different. It is a portal, a gateway between one world and the next. We can choose to walk through it, dragging the carcasses of our prejudice and hatred, our avarice, our data banks and dead ideas, our dead rivers and smoky skies behind us. Or we can walk through lightly, with little luggage, ready to imagine another world. And ready to fight for it.'

Let's work together to make the emergence from the pandemic the new birth moment for humankind; to create a world where we respect our planet, where we apply our creative energy to protecting the vulnerable and where we ensure that everyone, everywhere, should have a place to call home.

Epilogue
A story from the street – Sonny's story, in his own words

The Butcher of Gartnavel – the moment that changed my family forever

My name is Stuart 'Sonny' Murray. I was born in Glasgow in July 1979. In my early childhood, I had what I would consider to be a fairly typical upbringing. I lived with my mum, Moira, my dad, Raymond, and two brothers, Leon and Grant.

Our parents loved us and took good care of me and my brothers when we were kids. My dad had a good job in Glasgow Royal Infirmary as a mortuary technician and my mum was a housewife who focused on taking good care of the house and raising her sons. We grew up near Pollock in Glasgow, in a close-knit working-class community. I was best friends with my two brothers from a young age and we used to go and watch Glasgow Celtic play football regularly. Although we never had much, we were always a happy family and my brothers and I were generally content and well behaved.

Paying it Forward

There was no history of homelessness or addiction in my family and no reason to think that we wouldn't grow up to have happy and healthy lives.

My family's world was turned upside down in early 1980. At the time, I was only a baby when my family suffered one of the worst traumas imaginable. In his job at the mortuary at the Glasgow Royal Infirmary, my dad had a boss called James Harkins. As well as being his boss, James Harkins was also my dad's friend and the family would often see him and his wife, Joyce, in a social setting. In March 1980, something truly shocking and tragic happened that would affect my family forever and alter the course of my life from before I was even old enough to walk.

One day in a moment of madness, James killed his wife, son and his teenage brother-in-law. These horrific killings took place in a few moments of frenzy when James went to find Joyce at Gartnavel Hospital in Glasgow, where she worked as a nurse. Joyce had just finished her shift at work in the hospital and went to collect their son, James, from the crèche. Joyce's brother, Peter, had also come to the crèche to pick up his sister and her son and drive them home. James Harkins burst into the crèche with a scalpel that he had stolen from the mortuary and butchered his son, wife and brother-in-law, all in front of the screaming kids in the nursery. Joyce and James died with 23 stab wounds each. This tragic and shocking incident was widely reported in the UK media and James Harkins was branded 'The Butcher of Gartnavel'.

What was not so widely reported is that, directly after committing this horrific act of murder, and before he was arrested, James Harkins stole his brother-in-law's car and drove to our family home. In a rampage, he kicked down our front door and held me, my mum and my two brothers hostage. We were held captive for hours, which was all the more terrifying because he was still covered in blood from killing of his own family.

While I was too young to remember these terrifying few hours, thinking about the story that I heard from my mum still gives me chills. My mum managed to use the house phone to alert my dad to the fact we were all being held hostage by his unhinged boss. My dad had been at work and had already seen a newsflash on the television saying that three people had been killed at Gartnavel Hospital and the killer was on the run. Fearing for his family's lives, my dad came back to the house to try and get us to safety. He decided to get some back-up to help him, so he went to enlist the help of a local hardman named Frank Macatherty, who worked as a bouncer for the local off-licence. That was Glasgow for you back then – even the off-licences needed to have bouncers. My dad told Frank that he thought that James Harkins was the killer on the loose that the news was referring to and that he was currently in his home holding his wife and children hostage. With Frank's help, my dad set off to try and take James down.

When my dad and Frank arrived back at the house, it was already surrounded by armed police, who had tracked the stolen car back to our home. Initially the police refused to let my dad into the house, but when he became increasingly angry and demanded to go in first, the police obliged and let him and his friend Frank pass. My dad entered the house casually and told James that he and Frank were only coming in for a drink. Unbeknown to James, or to the police, Frank had hidden a hammer up his sleeve. When he went to shake hands with James, Frank instead revealed the hammer and struck James on the head, knocking him off balance. At this point, the armed police burst in and put guns to James's head, arrested him and took him to custody. That was it for James Harkins, and fortunately for everyone, he spent his life in Her Majesty's Prison and that is where he died.

While he was in prison and out of our lives forever, the wounds of trauma that he caused to my family on that day would never go away. Those few hours, when I was only a baby, would play a massive part in the path my life would go on to take. As you could imagine, my mum was completely traumatised by what happened and it affected her mental health desperately. She began to suffer from acute Post Traumatic Stress Disorder (PTSD) and despite her best efforts she was never really the same again. I am really proud of my mum for what she went through and how she tried her best to handle it. She was an amazing wee woman and she taught me a lot – mostly to be a good person and to look after people. The trauma and PTSD she suffered proved too much for her to handle and she developed a drug addiction to cope. At the time, there was no such thing as counselling or therapy in our community and my mum never really got the support she needed to move past this incident. Drugs won by default.

This traumatic experience and my mum's developing drug addiction put a strain on her marriage with my dad. Not long after, they separated and my dad disappeared from our lives before I was old enough to even remember him. I grew up without knowing my dad at all. In fact, I never met my dad again until I was 20 years old when I tracked him down after seeing him in the local paper. After my dad left, Mum got into another relationship with a man named Charlie. Charlie turned out to be really violent and abusive towards my mum. For most of my childhood, my abiding memories are of my mum and Charlie drinking and fighting. The stability and security of the family I was born into had disappeared and been replaced with poverty, violence and chaos. For most of my childhood, I have vivid memories of being hungry and unable to eat. It was shit.

Growing up in the care system

Eventually my two brothers and I got taken away from my mum and her abusive partner by social services and we were put into the care system. I can remember moving in with the first set of foster parents that we were assigned to in Glasgow. There were about another five wains, as well as me and my brothers, in the house. I remember one Easter we all got one Easter egg to share between about eight of us. Scarcity and hunger make up most of my memories of living in foster care. What's more, our foster parents used to be violent and hit us regularly.

After we got taken away from our mum, there was no sense of sanctuary for me or my brothers. As is fairly typical for children in the care system, you never really get the chance to feel settled because you are often bounced between different foster parents and children's homes.

After a few years of us living in different foster homes, my mum gave birth to a baby girl and I had a little sister. My mum managed to get herself clean and had left the violent relationship she was in with Charlie. She managed to regain custody of me and my brothers and we all moved into a Women's Aid shelter for women who had been suffering domestic abuse. This got us away from Glasgow and all the violence and poverty that had become so normal for us. The shelter we moved to was in a town called Bathgate in West Lothian, near Edinburgh. We were given a big five-bedroom home to live in together. It was amazing, just me, my mum and my siblings. I couldn't believe we had this house to ourselves and we were so thrilled to be reunited with our mum.

After a while, my mum's drug addiction issues resurfaced and my brothers and I started to misbehave. We became a bit of a law unto ourselves and we started refusing to go to school. After a long period of truancy, social services intervened again and this time my brother, Leon, and I got taken from our mum and put into a children's home in Edinburgh. As you can imagine, two Glaswegians in an Edinburgh children's home wasn't a lot of fun to start with. It felt like every day we were fighting – but if you fought one of us you would have to fight both of us. My brother and I had learned to look out for each other after going through such turmoil together. In order to make us attend school, we got placed in a residential school in Edinburgh. We were forced to attend school throughout the week and we were only allowed to go back and see our mum at the weekends.

Growing up through the care system, I learned a lot about how unsettling and traumatic it can be for young people who don't have a stable family background. I recently joined an advisory board of a charity called 'Who Cares? Scotland' to share my experiences of being in care to inform policy on how to improve the system. I love doing this sort of work and it gives me a sense of confidence. As

A story from the street - Sonny's story, in his own words

I was growing up, I knew I wanted to eventually get a job where I could help vulnerable people and I had hoped I could achieve this in my future.

Starting a family at 16 and finding drugs

While I was in the residential school, I met a girl called Lynne who was in my class, and we ended up starting a relationship. At the time, there was very little education about family planning or contraception. So, when we both left school at the age of 16, Lynne fell pregnant with my oldest son, Jamie. Lynne and I got a house together in an area called Wester Hailes in Edinburgh and I found a job in Edinburgh Zoo as a chef in the restaurant. Life was good and I was earning enough in my job as a chef to take good care of Lynne and my son. Three years later, Lynne fell pregnant again with our second son, Liam.

After Liam was born, cracks started to appear in my relationship with Lynne. We had been together since we were 14, and having two kids from such a young age without much support from our extended families put a lot of pressure on us. It reached a point where we were arguing so much that the relationship couldn't continue. Lynne asked me to leave so I agreed and moved back to my mum's house in Bathgate. Not long after this, my life became a bit chaotic and before long I had also lost my job at Edinburgh Zoo. At this point in my life, I started to go off the rails a bit. I had just lost the lassie who I had loved for years and was no longer seeing my two sons regularly. I had lost my house and my job – it really felt like everything that I had built up had gone almost overnight. To be honest, I felt absolutely devastated and I wasn't sure what to do next.

Paying it Forward

With my life seemingly at a dead end, I fell into a party scene and began taking drugs. I started with ecstasy, speed and cocaine. The sense of euphoria I found while I was high provided me with an escape. In order to feed my habit, I also started to sell drugs. My friend and I would go through to Glasgow and buy 100 ecstasy tablets for £3 each and then sell them in the nightclubs for £10 each. More than being addicted to the drugs, I became addicted to making money. I was only 19 years old and was walking out of the nightclub with £800 in my pocket every Friday and Saturday. We did this for about two years every single weekend and we used to celebrate our success by getting high at the clubs alongside our customers.

I gave up dealing drugs after two years when I met a girl called Pamela who I fell head over heels in love with. She told me that if I wanted to be with her then I would need to stop dealing. The money I was making and the euphoria of the drugs was no competition with Pamela, so meeting her meant the end of that chapter in my life. Plus, I figured it was only a matter of time before I would get caught by the police.

Pamela and Callan

After an amazing few years seeing Pamela, we had a son together called Callan, who is now 15 years old. Me, Pamela and Callan moved through to Airdrie where I was able to get away from all the drugs, police and all the other crap that I had become wrapped up in. I got myself a job and just got my head down to provide for my family. Airdrie was a rough wee place – it reminded me of being back in Glasgow. I was seeing plenty of violence on the streets, which gave me flashbacks from my childhood. The house we were moving into was in a rough estate where 'The Young Team' used to hang around. These were a gang of violent teenagers who roamed the estate drinking, taking drugs and generally causing trouble. I remember the graffiti that was on the wall of our house when we moved in saying, 'NO JUNKIES. NO GRASSES. NO BEASTS.', which I thought was fair enough! Despite the chaos going on around the estate, I just focused on being a family man. As well as looking after Callan, I started to see my first two sons, Jamie and Liam, every two weeks. We were a quiet wee family and everyone used to leave us alone. For the first time in a long time I felt happy and settled. But that wasn't to last for long.

My world came tumbling down again when I heard the news that my mum had died from a drug overdose. I was devastated by the news and fell into a pit of depression. I lost my job and started to turn to alcohol to cope with my emotions. Pamela didn't want me to be drinking so much around the wains, and after some months passed without my mental health improving, she couldn't cope with it any more and split up with me. This only led me to spiral further, and before I knew it, my ex-partner Lynne stopped bringing my older sons through to see me too. Much like with my childhood, in such a short space of time I went from feeling settled and happy to losing everything. It seemed like I never really had any safety net and any major shock in my life could throw the whole thing completely off balance.

Becoming homeless

I moved back to my mum's house in Bathgate. My wee sister was staying there too and my mum's death had hit her hard emotionally too. One night, when we were drinking, my sister and I got into an argument. The fight escalated into a screaming match. My sister ended up losing it, and picked up a kitchen knife and stabbed me seven times, puncturing both my lungs. I almost died and had to spend five days in hospital. My sister got charged with attempted murder but they had to drop the charges as I did not cooperate with the police. I knew my wee sister needed help, and I knew she would not get that in prison.

She had just lost her mum too and she was fucked up emotionally just like me. I wanted her to get another chance and to be able to recover from our mum's death.

Obviously when I got out of hospital I felt I couldn't go back to my mum's old house with my sister so I moved through to Edinburgh just to get away from everything and everyone. I didn't have any money or support network, so I found myself living on the streets. For the first time in my life, I was homeless. After a few nights finding shelter in doorways and alleyways, I met some other homeless people who showed me where a night shelter was, which was run by a charity called Streetwork. As well as a bed for the night, it was a place where I could have a shower, wash my clothes and get some food.

When I became homeless, I immediately felt a stigma from wider society. People walking past me on the street wouldn't even look me in the eyes – it felt like I had become invisible. My life was a real mess and I was regularly getting into trouble from the police for drinking on the street, shoplifting and other petty crimes. After repeat offences, I got sent to prison, which caused my life to spiral further out of control. For the first time in my life, when I was in jail, I was introduced to the drug heroin. I found myself sharing a cell with an older guy from Glasgow. One day he got a visit from his wife and when he came back he had a big bit of heroin on him. He was smoking this all night with the prison guards turning a blind eye. I had never taken heroin before and I had seen first-hand the destruction it caused in the communities I grew up in. When my cellmate offered me a smoke, I initially refused, knowing it was a path I did not want to go down. But he kept encouraging me to have just a few draws, telling me it would 'give me one night on the other side of the bars'. With my life already at as low an ebb as it could be, I figured that I had nothing much to lose. I took the joint from him and took a few draws. I sunk back into my single bed in our cell, took a deep breath and immediately forgot I was in jail. I forgot about what a mess my life was in. All the pain was immediately taken away.

After a few months, I was discharged from prison, leaving on a Friday night with nothing but a £40 discharge grant. I had no home to go to, so I made my way into Edinburgh and started sleeping on the streets again. This is a very common phenomenon for homeless people – living in a revolving door of the streets and prison. Without a safe place to call home, what chance did I have to get my life on track? Every day of my life was really uncertain, not knowing where I was going to sleep from one night to the next. I slept in shop doorways, and as the Scottish winter drew in, I would often shiver the night through. Sometimes I thought it would be good to get arrested again, just so I could get a roof over my head and three meals a day in prison. Occasionally I managed to get a place in the night shelter, which was a welcome reprieve from the cold. But in the shelters and hostels I found that drug addiction and bullying was rife. Each time I would leave the front door of the Salvation Army shelter on Holyrood Road, drug dealers would be waiting like predators – 'You want any gear, mate?' was a question that greeted me on a daily basis, multiple times a day.

Life became so depressing, cold and hopeless that after a while I started smoking heroin again. I knew I was being a right idiot, but I just wanted that sense of escape again from my reality – just like I had experienced in prison. Each day felt so precarious and scary that the only time I had a sense of peace was when I was high. My addiction soon spiralled and the purpose of each day became focused on scoring smack to smoke, and get a reprieve from my grim reality. The more I smoked, the deeper I sank into homeless-ness and the further I drifted from anything that was good in my life. It was a vicious cycle. I hadn't seen my wains in months and it started to seem impossible that I could ever get the things I hoped for in life – a home to call my own, a job, a sense of purpose and to see my children. Things quickly got really bad and I started to shoplift again to feed my habit.

When I was homeless and taking heroin, I met a girl called Biffy, who was in the same situation, and we started a relationship. It was good to have companionship on the street, but our relation-ship became destructive and toxic when Biffy started taking heroin with me. We used to go shoplifting together, sell what we stole and buy heroin. We would get high and find shelter on the streets of Edinburgh together.

Each day passed in what felt like Groundhog Day. We were stuck in a destructive loop and most days it felt like we were destined to live and die on the streets in a squalid existence. I was starting to lose all hope.

We were given a ray of light and the motivation to change our lives when Biffy fell pregnant. We were sick of living this lifestyle, and although the physical and emotional withdrawals of coming off heroin would be horrendous, we knew we had to make a change. We were bringing a new life into the world. When Biffy was almost due to give birth, I found myself in court for shoplifting offences again. I was just about to get remanded in prison and I knew this would ruin my chances of getting my life back on track and keep me in the rut I was in. So, out of pure desperation, I decided to speak up for myself in the dock to the judge. When I started to speak, the judge encouraged me to keep going, saying he wanted to hear what I had to say. I told the judge the truth. I said that I was a heroin addict and I was sick of the lifestyle. I told him that my girlfriend Biffy was pregnant and I wanted to change my life so I could be a father. I told the judge that it was in one of his prisons that I first tried heroin and going back to prison was not the place for me to find rehabilitation. I broke down in tears in the dock and pleaded with the judge for help. He listened intently to me, shaking his head in disbelief when he heard that prison was where I was first introduced to heroin.

The judge decided to give me a chance. He gave me bail for a DTTO (Drug Treatment and Testing Order) assessment. This meant that I would get put on a prescription and see a drugs worker twice a week, instead of going to prison. I had been given a lifeline to turn my life around.

I decided I wanted to try and get a job before Biffy gave birth. I wanted to earn a steady wage but more importantly to give myself something to focus on every day to keep me on a good path. I was living in homeless accommodation and with my criminal record and history of drug abuse it was almost impossible to find an employer that would trust me enough to give me a job. I handed in a CV to hundreds of businesses in Edinburgh but I didn't get one single job offer. When you have a history of homelessness and prison, there really is no such thing as 'social mobility'. Without any other options, in order to try and get money to eat, day to day, I started begging on the streets. I would sit on North Bridge in Edinburgh in the freezing cold and was grateful if I could scrape £5 together from the passing public throwing some change into my hat.

Social Bite, Charlotte, George Clooney and turning things around

One day, when I was sitting on the street, shivering through a cold winter's day, I was offered a ray of light. A young man approached me and asked if I had heard of a cafe called 'Social Bite'. The young man was Jack Littlejohn, who was the younger brother of the co-founder of the cafe, Josh. Jack told me that the cafe was offering free food and jobs to homeless people and encouraged me to go along. I had never heard of any cafe like this, so I decided to wander over and see if it was too good to be true. I walked to their cafe on Rose Street and, to my amazement, they offered me a free cup of tea and a sandwich. It felt nice to be able to go into a cafe like a regular person and be greeted with eye contact and a warm smile.

After going in for free food for a few weeks, I built up the courage to go in and ask for a job. I went in and spoke to the founders, Josh and Alice, and told them my situation. I explained that I was

A story from the street – Sonny's story, in his own words

homeless but that my girlfriend had a baby on the way and I was determined to turn my life around. I obviously presented a big risk for their new business so initially they got me to hand out leaflets to promote the cafe for two hours a day. They wanted to see if I could be reliable and turn up every day without being under the influence of drugs or alcohol. After a few weeks of handing out the leaflets without any issues, they told me to keep up the hard work and when a full-time job became available it would be mine. True to their word, about three weeks later I was working full-time. I was given different roles, serving customers in the cafe and preparing the food in their central kitchen in Livingston. I loved the sense of purpose and earning a steady wage. It also felt good to help the other people who were coming into the cafes for free food. For once I was the helper rather than the charity case. The stability of the job enabled me to get my own flat in Fountainbridge in Edinburgh, and for the first time in a long time I felt hopeful about my future. Before long, Biffy gave birth to our beautiful daughter, Charlotte.

I am delighted to say that this was seven years ago and today Charlotte is a gorgeous, healthy little girl, settled in at primary school. Biffy and I are still going strong as a couple – both holding down our own separate tenancies. Furthermore, I am now a qualified tour guide in Edinburgh too. Over the last seven years, my life has totally changed and I have done things that I would never have dreamed possible. Each year, I have been invited to Josh's Scottish Business Awards event so we get to meet amazing people like President Bill Clinton and Sir Richard Branson. One year the Scottish Olympic legend Sir Chris Hoy was attending the event and he bought me a drink! I remember thinking, *Wow,*

this time last year I was in prison and addicted to heroin – now I'm
standing at the bar having a beer with Sir Chris Hoy. I used to not
have enough warm clothes to get me through a winter's night on
the streets; I can't believe that I have now got three brand-new
suits to my name!

Definitely my best day with Social Bite was meeting George
Clooney when he came to the cafe. I even had the chance to tell
him about my life and he just listened and laughed and joked with
me, before encouraging me for the future. Since then I have met
Leonardo DiCaprio, Prince Harry and Meghan Markle, Malala
Yousafzai, the Nobel Peace Prize winner, and loads of other amazing people. I never thought I would mix with the rich and famous,
but I am always amazed how interested they all are in my story.

I am now a spokesperson throughout Scotland on the issue of
homelessness. I give public talks about my experience of being on
the streets and how we could improve things for homeless people.
I have spoken in front of 8,000 people at an event and I have given
speeches at many business conferences. I am also planning to give a
TEDx Talk next year.

I am also a tour guide in Edinburgh. I am a guide with another
social enterprise called 'Invisible Cities' where we show tourists
some sights in Edinburgh but we also show them the underbelly
of the city and things they wouldn't get to see on traditional tours.
The theme of my tour is Crime and Punishment, which, given my
track record is pretty appropriate! Alongside popular tourist spots
like the Edinburgh Dungeons and the Royal Mile, I also show the
tourists where I used to sleep on the streets and highlight the amazing charities that help vulnerable people in the city.

A story from the street – Sonny's story, in his own words

When I look back at my life I understand how any of our lives can change in an instant. I often think that if James Harkins had never held my family hostage that day, then my mum would not have suffered the trauma she did and I would have probably had a stable and happy life. If I had never shared a cell with a heroin addict, I would never have gone down that path and ended up in such a desperate situation. But at the same time, I never could have dreamed when I was growing up in poverty in Glasgow that I would be on CNN News in America with George Clooney or be interviewed by the *New York Times* about homelessness. In the same way your life can change negatively in an instant, it can also change in amazing ways. I feel like I have been given a second chance at life and I am loving it. I obviously still have problems like everyone else in life and I am sure I always will. But I know my future is bright as I will continue to be there for all of my kids, embrace new experiences and give homeless and vulnerable people a voice whenever I tell my story.

Peace. Xxx

Acknowledgements

My journey as a social entrepreneur has been supported by so many amazing people over the years, some of whom I would love to take the opportunity to acknowledge and thank here.

Firstly, I would like to thank my wife, Sukhi, for all of her love and support throughout the good times and the bad – supporting me to overcome the many challenges that life as a social entrepreneur has thrown at me. Many of these have could have had a big impact on our personal lives and, during these times, you have been incredible. I would like to thank my parents for giving me the love, support and foundation to build the life that I chose. Dad: thank you for always teaching me that I can achieve whatever I set my mind to. Mum: thank you for being so invested in my journey and supporting me every step of the way with such love. Joanie, Graham, Charan and Manjit: thank you for always listening to my challenges and supporting me at every turn.

Paying it Forward

Thank you to my brother, Jack, who, as well as being a brilliant brother, also was extremely influential in helping Social Bite get off the ground, from painting the first shop to pushing himself to breaking point as the area manager of the cafes in the early years. All to help me out as a brother.

Social Bite has had many fantastic board members over the years, who have all volunteered their time and who have been a huge support to both the charity and to me personally. I would like to thank Angus Morrison for all the time, energy and support you have given, and for which I will always be grateful. Thank you to William Gorol for investing over 10 years as a chairperson and trustee of Social Bite – without you the charity would never have survived and thrived, and I am so grateful for everything you have done, not to mention for coming back to provide invaluable support in recent years. Thank you to Sir Andrew Cubie for your leadership in guiding Social Bite through the significant challenges we have faced as our indefatigable chairman, and for the considerable time you have given up to do so. Thank you to the late Daniel Muir who was our first ever chairperson and played a critical role in bringing the Social Bite Village project to life. Thank you to Marjory Rodger for the decade's worth of energy that you invested into Social Bite: the charity would not have become what it is without you. Thank you to Katie Crook for the time you have shared with us chairing our trading business and, now, for your support as a trustee. And thank you to all the other board members who have given up their valuable time and commitment over the years – and still do. Each and every contribution is very much valued.

Acknowledgements

Thank you to Social Bite's co-founder, Alice Thompson, who invested so much time and energy to help launch and build the charity, and who has now gone on to launch her own successful coaching business. Thank you to Alan Mahon, who was my right-hand man in staging the Scottish Business Awards events, and who went on to launch and build a fantastic social enterprise called Brewgooder.

Thank you to our marvellous team who have taken the cause of Social Bite to their hearts and made it into the organisation it is today. To Louise, Sara, Jamie, Marzena, Peter, Mel, Lucy, Jen, Natasha, Ross, Babs, Emma, Euan, Ambreen, Alessio, Elaine, Mary, Paul, Joanna, Inna, Elaine, Awena, Gemma, Danny, Aaron, Mikey, Matteo, Scott, Cameron, Matthew, and everyone else – thank you for everything you do for Social Bite each and every day!

Thank you to the various people that I have met from homeless backgrounds who inspired Social Bite's journey, and who continue to inspire me. Particularly to Pete, Joe, Colin, and Sonny: thanks for being inspirations and good friends for over 10 years.

Thank you to our donors and supporters, who are too numerous to mention all by name, but I would like to take the opportunity to acknowledge a few. In particular, a big thank you to Hamid Guedroudj, who is the most generous philanthropist I have known and who has been the primary supporter of Social Bite's projects throughout our history, as well as The World's Big Sleepout campaign. Without Hamid we would have never survived or realised any of the dreams I had for the organisation. Thank you, Hamid and Faiza, for everything you have done.

Thank you also for the unbelievable support over the years to a range of inspirational and generous supporters. In particular to Alan Parker and the Oak Foundation, Bruce Wishart, Andy Lothian, David Wither, Tom Tracy, Bill Dobbie, Sir Peter Vardy, Stephen McCranor, Shaf Rasul, John Watson, Dean Gassabi, Brian McRitchie, Dame Louise Casey, Caryl Stern, Sir Tom Hunter, Sir Brian Souter, Ian Marchant, Richard Curtis, Jason Iley, Mark Ross, Abid Faqir, Alan McLeish, Phyllis McLeish, Caroline and Steve Halliday and the Castansa Trust, Susan Bitker, WM Sword Trust, Paul Brooks, Chris Van Der Kuyl and Paddy Burns, Bob Keiller, David Dinsmore, Jim Law, Jennifer Cheyne, Geoff Ellis, People's Postcode Lottery, Google, Rockstar Games, Oli Norman and Itison, Graeme Watt and the team at Softcat, Alastair Storey and BaxterStorey, Martin Armstrong and Wheatley Group, Beth Knight and Amazon UK, James Clarry, Peter Flavel, Alison Rose and the teams at Coutts and the NatWest Group, David Duffy and Virgin Money UK, Richard Houston and the team at Deloitte, Chris Reeve and the team at PwC, Alan Jope and Unilever, Conor O'Leary and Gleneagles Hotel, Jane Rawnsley and M&G, Stuart Turnbull and the team at Jacobs, Chris Rae and all at CMS, the teams at Just Eat, Mitchells & Butlers, Arup, Addleshaw Goddard, Ooni, Mackie's of Scotland, Sky Cares, Albert Hunt Trust and W A Cargill Charitable Trust – not to mention many more too numerous to mention here.

Thank you to also to key supporters of the Social Bite Village not mentioned above, who were instrumental in making it a reality, including Gill Henry and Cruden Group, Matt Stevenson, Tony Hackney and BSW Timber, Bill and Elliot Robertson and all at the Robertson Group, FES Group, Murray McCall and all at Anderson Strathern, Bruce Mickel and the Mickel family,

Acknowledgements

Jonathan Avery, PYC, Fouin and Bell Architects, Will Rudd Davidson, Pottie Wilson, Peter Graham, The Keenan Consultancy, Wardell Armstrong, Cornhill Building Services, Scottish Water, Clancy Docwra, Homer, Openreach, Mason Evans, Douglas Land Surveys, Nigel Rudd Ecology, Norbord, JTC Furniture Group, Thornbridge Sawmills, Caledonian Plywood, Colinson Ceramics, Spirit of Wood, Howdens Joinery, John Brodie and all at Scotmid and John and Norman Scott and the Scott Group.

Thank you to Adrian Sington and all at Kruger Cowne, as well as my publisher, Rik Ubhi, and all at Bonnier Books for their support in bringing this book to life and making it happen. It has been a pleasure to work with you all on *Paying It Forward*.

And, last but not least, to everyone else who has been involved in my journey over the years, whether you have donated to Social Bite, bought a sandwich, volunteered, or in any other way 'paid it forward'. Thank you to each and every one of you. I'll hopefully see you all down the road.

Notes and References

Introduction

'Billionaires added $5 trillion to their fortunes during the pandemic', Anna Cooban, CNN Business, 16 January 2022: https://edition.cnn.com/2022/01/16/business/oxfam-pandemic-davos-billionaires/index.html

'Richest 1% bag nearly twice as much wealth as the rest of the world put together over the past two years', OXFAM International, 16 January 2023: https://www.oxfam.org/en/press-releases/richest-1-bag-nearly-twice-much-wealth-rest-world-put-together-over-past-two-years

'At least 271,000 people are homeless in England today', Shelter, 11 January 2023: https://england.shelter.org.uk/media/press_release/at_least_271000_people_are_homeless_in_england_today

'Forced displacement at record 68.5 million', Adrian Edwards, The UN Refugee Agency, 19 June 2018: https://www.unhcr.org/uk/news/stories/forced-displacement-record-68-5-million

Paying it Forward

'Pending Global Recession Could See Homelessness Increase to Great Depression Levels', Cynthia Griffith, Invisible People, 9 January 2023: https://invisiblepeople.tv/pending-global-recession-could-see-homelessness-increase-to-great-depression-levels/

Chapter 1

'Steve Jobs and his remarkably simple secret of life', Peter Economy, Inc.com, 18 June 2015: https://www.inc.com/peter-economy/steve-jobs-on-the-1-remarkably-simple-secret-of-life.html

'All about Social Enterprise', Social Enterprise UK, 4 June 2023: https://www.socialenterprise.org.uk/all-about-social-enterprise

'There are 471,000 social enterprises in the UK, government report finds', Alice Sharman, Civil Society, accessed 1 June 2023: https://www.civilsociety.co.uk/news/there-are-471-000-social-enterprises-in-the-uk-government-report-finds.html

'Social Business', Muhammad Yunus, Yunus Centre, 8 January 2020: https://www.muhammadyunus.org/post/2113/social-business

'American CEOs make 351 times more than workers. In 1965 it was 15 to one', Indigo Olivier, *Guardian*, 17 August 2021: https://www.theguardian.com/commentisfree/2021/aug/17/ american-chief-executive-pay-wages-workers

'Top FTSE 100 bosses earn 117 times average UK workers', Oscar Williams-Grut, Yahoo! Finance, accessed 1 June 2023: https://uk.finance.yahoo.com/news/ceo-pay-ftse-100-cipd-high-pay-centre-117-average-worker-230131187.html

Notes and References

'The boss who put everyone on 70k', Stephanie Hegarty, BBC
News, 28 February 2020: https://www.bbc.co.uk/news/
stories-51332811

Chapter 2

'Do We Need $75,000 a Year to Be Happy?', Belinda Luscombe, *TIME*,
6 September 2010: https://content.time.com/time/magazine/
article/0%2C9171%2C2019628%2C00.html
'The Reason Many Ultrarich People Aren't Satisfied With Their
Wealth', Joe Pinkser, the *Atlantic*, 4 September 2018: https://
www.theatlantic.com/family/archive/2018/12/rich-people-
happy-money/577231/

Chapter 5

'A Theory of Human Motivation', A.H Maslow (1943), originally
publishing in *Psychological Review*, 50, 370-396, reproduced in
Classics in the History of Psychology, York University, accessed
1 June 2023: https://psychclassics.yorku.ca/Maslow/motivation.
htm

Chapter 7

'The homeless workers taking on Greggs, Eat and Pret a
Manger', Adam Forrest, *Guardian*, 25 March 2015: https://
www.theguardian.com/sustainable-business/2015/mar/25/
homeless-edinburgh-work-jobs-poverty-employment-
greggs-pret
Murray, William H., *The Scottish Himalayan Expedition*, London:
Dent, 1951, p.7

Chapter 8

'George Clooney cheered at Edinburgh café that helps homeless people', Libby Brooks, *Guardian*, 12 November 2015: https://www.theguardian.com/film/2015/nov/12/george-clooney-visit-edinburgh-social-bites-cafe-helps-homeless-people

'Leonardo DiCaprio highlights plight of homeless in Social Bite restaurant visit', *Herald*, 16 November 2016: https://www.heraldscotland.com/news/14908872.leonardo-dicaprio-highlights-plight-homeless-social-bite-restaurant-visit/

Chapter 12

'Basic Facts About Homelessness: New York City', Coalition for the Homeless, February 2023: https://www.coalitionforthehomeless.org/basic-facts-about-homelessness-new-york-city/

'"We have failed"': how California's homelessness catastrophe is worsening, Sam Levin, *Guardian*, 22 March 2022: https://www.theguardian.com/us-news/2022/mar/22/california-homelessness-crisis-unhoused-and-unequal

'Informal Settlements', Economic and Social Council, Lilien Nagy, ed. Márton Levente Sipos and Csanád Végh, Karinthy Model United Nations, Budapest, Hungary, 2019: https://karmun.hu/images/issues/ECOSOC_informal_settlements.pdf

Chapter 15

'Muhammad Ali: In his own words', CBS News, 5 June 2016: https://www.cbsnews.com/news/muhammad-ali-in-his-own-words/

'Affordable Housing, Inclusive Economic Policies Key to Ending Homelessness, Speakers Say as Social Development

Notes and References

Begins Annual Session', United Nations, 10 February
2020: https://press.un.org/en/2020/soc4884.doc.
htm#:~:text=Globally%2C%201.6%20billion%20people%20
live,Programme%20(UN%2DHabitat)
'What is IGH?', Ruff Institute of Global Homelessness, 1 June 2023
https://ighhub.org/about-us
'Address at the Sorbonne in Paris, France: "Citizenship in a
Republic"' (23 April, 1910), The American Presidency Project, UC
Santa Barbara, accessed 1 June 2023: https://www.presidency.
ucsb.edu/documents/address-the-sorbonne-paris-france-
citizenship-republic

Chapter 16

'Extreme inequality and essential services', Oxfam International,
accessed 1 June 2023: https://www.oxfam.org/en/what-we-do/
issues/extreme-inequality-and-essential-services
'The pandemic is a portal', Arundhati Roy, Financial Times, 3 April
2020: https://www.ft.com/content/10d8f5e8-74eb-11ea-95fe-
fcd274e920ca
'A letter from Professor Muhammad Yunus', Muhammad Yunus,
LinkedIn, 5 April 2020: https://www.linkedin.com/pulse/letter-
from-professor-muhammad-yunus-super-hapyyness-festival-
yunus